Pelican Books
Taxation Policy

W. A. Robson and Bernard Crick are joint editors
of the *Political Quarterly*, which was founded
in 1930 with Robson and Kingsley Martin (who
was soon succeeded by Leonard Woolf) as
joint editors. The *Political Quarterly* has been an
influential journal of public policy for forty years,
always striving to bridge the gap between theory
and practice, the specialist and the generalist,
and the universities and Whitehall.

William Robson is Professor Emeritus of Public
Administration in London University and author
of *Nationalised Industry and Public Ownership*
and *Local Government in Crisis* among many other
works.

Professor Bernard Crick is head of the joint
department of Politics and Sociology at Birkbeck
College, London, and author of *In Defence of
Politics* (also a Pelican book) and *The Reform of
Parliament* among other writings.

Taxation Policy

Edited for the *Political Quarterly*
by William A. Robson and Bernard Crick

Penguin Books

Penguin Books Ltd, Harmondsworth,
Middlesex, England
Penguin Books Inc., 7110 Ambassador Road,
Baltimore, Maryland 21207, U.S.A.
Penguin Books Australia Ltd, Ringwood,
Victoria, Australia

This collection first published 1973
Copyright © *Political Quarterly*, 1972

Made and printed in Great Britain by
Cox & Wyman Ltd, London, Reading and Fakenham
Set in Intertype Plantin

Contents

I

The Political Economy of Taxation

WILLIAM A. ROBSON

We have attempted in this symposium to look more broadly at taxation policy than ministers, MPs, Civil Servants or political parties are wont to do. It sets out the views of a dozen writers who are well qualified by virtue of their political, economic, administrative or academic knowledge and experience to contribute to this difficult subject. It is not intended to be a textbook, although it will doubtless be widely read by students of public finance and fiscal problems.

The topics our contributors discuss comprise what we regard as the most vital aspects of taxation policy: they include the effects of taxation on the poor and on the rich; its influence on incentives and on economic growth; national insurance contributions considered as part of our system of taxation; changes which could with advantage be introduced into taxes on income, capital gains, gifts, and inheritance; and the part which the House of Commons could and should play in scrutinizing and debating taxation policy. Value-added tax receives the attention it deserves.

There are, however, a number of topics which we have deliberately left out of this book. Among them are the incidence of local rates, means-tested benefits, the system of allowances for income tax, family allowances, negative income tax, the existing system of indirect taxes, company taxation, the taxation of charities, taxation in relation to works of art, the cost and efficiency of administrative methods employed in collecting taxes. These and other topics might all be appropriate for a textbook but not for a symposium such as this, which concentrates on stimulating thought about key problems rather than on comprehensive coverage of 'the subject'.

A topic we have deliberately avoided is a comparison between the level of taxation in Britain and that in other industrialized countries. Such a comparison is meaningless unless it brings into the picture not only the burdens but also the benefits received. To equate the vast range of services rendered by governments in cash or in kind, from defence to highways, education, personal medical services, town planning, housing and all the rest, and to quantify them in monetary terms in a comparative table, would take many years of investigation and calculation. In the absence of such calculations any statement about Britain being more or less heavily taxed than some other country or countries is of dubious validity.

Everyone will agree that taxation is a matter of prime importance. It has profound economic, social and political effects on our lives as individual citizens and as a nation. Yet despite its unquestionable importance, taxation policy is never officially considered in a comprehensive manner. The Chancellor of the Exchequer for the time being introduces piecemeal changes such as the capital-gains tax or selective employment tax without any regard for the tax system as a whole. There has not been within living memory a select committee, Royal Commission or other public inquiry into our system of taxation in its entirety. Yet this is what matters in the end, rather than the effects of this or that tax.

Mr Barber in his 1971 budget speech proposed more reforms than any Chancellor of the Exchequer who has held office this century. Among the notable improvements which he announced were the replacement of income tax and surtax by a single graduated income tax; the removal of the absurd arrangement whereby a married couple pays more tax than two single persons with the same earnings; the merging of short-term capital gains with long-term capital gains; the repeal of the legislation which taxes the investment income of young children as though it were the income of their parents; the removal of tax discrimination against investment income up to a certain figure to be specified; the equalization of corporate taxation as between distributed and undistributed profits; the limitation on the marginal rates of taxation on very high incomes to a maximum of 75 per cent; and the eventual replacement of purchase tax and selective employment tax by value-added taxes.

This considerable programme of reform was a remarkable and commendable effort by Mr Barber, but no one could claim that it was comprehensive. This indeed is shown by the fact that the defects set out in the chapters of this book, most of which were written before the budget speech, are untouched by the Chancellor's proposals, despite the fact that some of his changes seek to remedy injustices, while others may encourage savings and promote investment. This only serves to show how many-faceted is the subject of taxation.

Taxes were originally devised in order to provide the revenue necessary to pay for functions performed by the state. This is still a major objective, but it is nowadays only one among several aims. Other purposes are demand management, redistribution of income or wealth, economic growth, discrimination between certain types of goods and services as regards both production and consumption, and encouragement of exports or discouragement of imports. There is an unfortunate tendency to mix up all these purposes, so that one never knows what purpose or purposes a particular tax or the tax system as a whole is intended to serve, and in what order of importance. Mr Brittan points out in his essay that the desire for collective spending does not necessarily go hand in hand with a desire for a more equitable distribution of income; but as things are at present the egalitarian argument inevitably implies more taxation and increased collective expenditure. He proposes that the question of the level of public expenditure should be separated from the question of the amount of redistribution we wish to see brought about in the community. He also rejects the notion, so sedulously cultivated by Mr Heath's Government, that a cut in taxation represents a genuine saving in expenditure by the citizen. Thus the budgetary saving resulting from replacing deficiency payments to farmers by levies on food imports is entirely spurious, since what the citizen saves in taxes will be counteracted by the higher prices he has to pay for food in the shops.

There are four basic questions which may properly be asked respecting taxation, apart from the question whether it produces sufficient revenue to pay for the services provided by the government with the consent of Parliament. These questions concern the effect of taxation on incentives, on the distribution of income and wealth, on economic growth and on the administrative efficiency of the system.

Transcending the practical questions of fiscal policy are some moral issues which take us into a higher realm of discourse. It is very unusual for a philosopher to turn his attention to the ethics of taxation, and we welcome the attempt by Professor Raphael to turn the searchlight of political philosophy on to the moral problems of fiscal policy. He emphasizes the difference of outlook between people who base moral rights on merit and those who base them on equality and need. The welfare state is founded on the belief in social justice, about which there is a broad consensus of opinion in Britain today, at least so far as the satisfaction of primary human needs is concerned. But there is no agreement about how far the concept of social justice should be applied in taxation policy; and philosophy cannot answer this question. What the philosopher can do is to make clear the nature of the issues.

Professor Raphael analyses the distinction between justice and utility in the aims of taxation, and shows how they can in some circumstances be reconciled under the general formula of distributive justice; but this requires that utility be associated with merit. Often, however, justice in meeting needs does nothing to promote social utility, and it is here that we may find serious clashes of opinion between the socialist and his conservative opponents. Professor Raphael does not put forward a programme of reform but he does point out the need to link taxation policy with an incomes policy. His general conclusion is that the ethical position of socialists and radicals is more widely acceptable and theoretically justified than it sometimes appears to be.

There is a widespread belief in this country that the level of income tax (including surtax) is so high that it has seriously weakened the desire or the will to work. This view is supported by Sir Richard Clarke, who points out that the progression of taxation is the steepest in the world for those possessing the top 2 per cent of personal incomes. He is in no doubt that persons in that category have huge incentives to engage in tax avoidance – a quite legitimate activity – in respect both of their incomes and estates. A vast amount of highly skilled professional talent and brain-power is diverted into this sterile occupation. Moreover, he is of the opinion that the tax system undoubtedly produces disincentives to increased work and the taking of risks, from which the whole economy suffers. There is, however, no hard evidence on the subject applicable to present-day conditions, and the authors of a recent study reviewing the evidence declare that the only intellectually honest answer to the question 'Do direct taxes have a disincentive effect?' is 'No'.[1] Professor Peston traces in his article the complexity of this question, and shows that what constitutes an incentive to one man may act as a disincentive to another. He also stresses the many other factors which influence the work output of individuals. Indeed, the whole question of the limits of taxable capacity is shrouded in mystery at the present time. One can safely assume that much depends on the purpose or purposes for which taxation is levied or thought to be levied; the forms which it takes; the incidence as between individuals and classes; and the effect on accustomed standards of living.

Belief in the disincentive effect of income tax is very often based on the steep progression in the rates of surtax falling on high incomes. Mr Piachaud shows that direct taxation begins at levels substantially below the poverty line recognized by the Supplementary Benefits Commission, despite the principle enunciated by a Royal Commission in 1954 that income tax should not be levied on any income which is insufficient to provide the recipient with subsistence at a level to sustain health and efficiency. The figures in his article reveal that many men and women in full-time employment are forced to live below the poverty line because of their liability to income tax and national

1. C. V. Brown and D. A. Dawson, *Personal Taxation Incentives and Tax Reform*, PEP Broadsheet 506, 1969, p. 66.

insurance contributions. Quite apart from this is the fact that the marginal tax rates from these two sources are very high for a large number of ordinary wage-earning families. Thus, a man with 2 children of 8 and 10 years old earning £18 a week will have a marginal tax-rate of 80 per cent. If his wages rise to £19 his net income will go up only from £15.25 to £15.45. A 4-child family earning £20 a week may have a marginal tax-rate of 130 per cent, so that a rise of £1 a week will bring about a reduction of net income from £19.70 to £19.40.

After considering such adverse facts as these, Mr Piachaud considers possible methods of relieving the poverty which still exists on a substantial scale in our society, and which is exacerbated by such high marginal rates of tax and the taxation of families living below the poverty line. He considers various remedies such as negative income tax, social dividend flat-rate payments, and a national minimum wage, but rejects each in turn on political, economic or psychological grounds. He does not believe it to be politically feasible to bring about any large-scale relief of poverty by means of income redistribution effected through taxation.

It is probably for this reason that attention is beginning to be paid to wealth taxes in one form or another. Professor Atkinson gives figures to show that capital wealth in Britain is still concentrated in a small proportion of the population. There has been a considerable redistribution during this century, but the shift has been mainly, though not entirely, from the very rich to the rich. He criticizes the present system of estate duty mainly because it has so slight an effect on redistributing wealth. He distinguishes inherited wealth from the accumulation of savings during a person's lifetime, and contends that death duties should not fall, as they do at present, on the testator but rather on the beneficiary. An essential feature of his scheme is the proposal to aggregate all the gifts and legacies received by an individual during his lifetime in order to impose progressive rates of inheritance tax on the recipient. His scheme has unquestionable advantages over an annual wealth tax, which would be extremely difficult to administer in practice, and which would fail to distinguish between inherited wealth and wealth accumulated during a man's lifetime.

Professor Sandford looks carefully at the advantages and disadvantages of the death duties we now have. They arouse less hostility from tax-payers as a means of diminishing inequality and bring about less economic disturbance than a wealth tax or a capital levy would be likely to do. When one asks about their effect on incentives to save, we come up once more against a blank wall of ignorance. It is possible that heavy death duties may discourage some people from saving while stimulating others to save more than they otherwise would. Professor Sandford shares the view expressed by Professor Atkinson that if the main purpose is to reduce inequalities, an inheritance tax would be far more effective than estate duty. He emphasizes that it is large bequests rather than large estates which perpetuate inequality. A progressive inheritance-tax would probably provide an incentive to rich men to distribute their wealth more widely in their wills in order to reduce the total burden of taxation falling on the estate and on the recipients. Our present rates of estate duty may be the highest in the world; but the liability to pay them is more easily avoided by gifts *inter vivos* than in other countries – not a very sensible method of dealing with the situation. A gifts tax could be easily integrated with an inheritance tax and should be an essential feature of any attempt to reduce inequality among the owners of property.

Professor Clayton and Mr Houghton propose to deal with gifts, inheritance, gambling winnings and other adventitious accretions of property by means of a drastic reform of the income-tax system. All such additions would be treated as income, thereby diminishing the need for a tax on wealth, but in order to avoid the unfairness caused by 'bunching' they would be averaged over a period of at least 5 years. These authors suggest many other radical changes, such as the abolition of the higher personal allowance for married men, which they criticize as an anachronism; the payment of family allowances for the second

13

child at a higher rate than for subsequent children; removal of the discrimination between earned and unearned income; and the introduction of tax loans and deferred tax payments.

A feature of our system of direct taxation to which Sir Richard Clarke draws attention is the remarkable difference between the relative position of families and of single persons within the same income bracket. This seems to have attracted little notice except in regard to the poorest families. He points out that the difference between the standard of living of those with dependents compared with those without is at least as great at middle-class income levels as at the lower levels. Vertical comparisons overlook this phenomenon entirely, and it can only be brought into the limelight by horizontal comparisons.

Perhaps too much emphasis is placed in Britain on the redistributive aspect of taxation and too little attention given to its potential influence on economic growth. To be fair to Mr Heath, he has repeatedly said that he regards a reduction of taxation as an incentive to economic growth, and reduced corporation tax as a means of increasing the industrial investment which is a necessary condition of expansion. This view was echoed by Mr Barber in his budget speech. The relation between taxation and growth is the theme of Professor Prest's contribution, and he makes no attempt to conceal the difficulty and the complexity of the subject. Here again there is a remarkable lack of precise knowledge, and the author is sceptical about the soundness of inquiries which have tended to show that tax variables have little effect on investment decisions. One advantage of the value-added tax is that it is a tax which exempts investment and falls either on consumption or alternatively on wages and salaries. Professor Prest thinks a case can be made out for tax discrimination between industries, regions and occupations, but he has serious doubts about the success of selective employment tax in stimulating the output of manufactured goods.

Professor Prest agrees with Professor Peston that it has not been proved that our high marginal rates of tax serve as an important deterrent to work, but he thinks nevertheless that they cannot be defended in view of the lower trends in North America.

He is presumably thinking of the brain-drain which is the ultimate defence against oppressive or penal taxation. It applies to business entrepreneurs and managers no less than to doctors and scientists.

Our fiscal policy in recent years does not show up well in terms of economic growth. In some of the OECD countries taxation has helped to increase the rate of growth while in others it has had no such effect. In the United Kingdom fiscal policy has intensified fluctuations, whereas it was a stabilizing force in the United States.

The general conclusion at which Professor Prest arrives is that there are severe limits to the influence which fiscal policy can have on economic growth and that selective intervention by means of taxation must be approached with great caution.

National insurance contributions are referred to in passing by some of the authors: Mr Piachaud points out that they are like taxes insofar as they are imposed compulsorily, and Mr Brittan in his appendix explains that the gross outgoings of the national insurance funds are included in the Treasury definition of public expenditure. Professor Abel-Smith devotes the whole of his essay to a close examination of social security considered from the standpoint of taxation. The starting point of his argument is the need to deal with the substantial problem of poverty which is still with us. If we took less from poor families at work we should not need to give them so much to relieve their poverty. 'To take less is as blessed as to give more,' he remarks, 'indeed, more blessed insofar as less stigma attaches to retaining what one has earned than to receiving what one has not.' The heaviest burden at present placed on the poor consists of national insurance contributions which are largely devoted to relieving destitution among those not at work – the sick, the unemployed, the disabled. In levying these contributions, ability to pay is almost ignored and, unlike contributions to occupational pension schemes, mortgage payments and life-insurance premiums, they cannot even be deducted in assessing liability to income tax.

The flat-rate system of national insurance is now on its way out, and will eventually be replaced by a scheme in which both

15

contributions and benefits are related to earnings. The Labour Government's Bill, introduced by Mr Crossman, differentiated in favour of the lower income levels and especially those below the poverty line. The present Conservative Government shares this intention to move towards an income-related scheme and has already made a substantial move in that direction. The new level of contributions is less regressive than the old, but it still takes a higher proportion of the earnings of the lowest-paid worker compared with those in the higher brackets. Professor Abel-Smith contends that the purpose of the Exchequer contribution to the national insurance fund should be reconsidered, and he urges that this sum of over £500 million a year could and should be used to subsidize the contributions of the lower-paid workers.

Hitherto, there has been a discernible relationship between contributions and benefits which has done much to ensure the acceptability and credibility of the 'insurance' principle among the great body of wage-earners. Indeed, it is this which distinguishes insurance contributions from taxes. Now, Professor Abel-Smith writes, this basic principle is challenged by Sir Keith Joseph's decision to finance flat-rate benefits by earnings-related contributions. He thinks that this change may undermine the whole system of national insurance and create resistance to the payment of contributions which had not previously existed while the 'insurance' myth persisted among the general public.

Mr Mackintosh takes us into the parliamentary arena and puts the case for allowing the House of Commons to inquire into and scrutinize taxation policy either by means of a select committee on the subject or through a select committee on economic affairs. This was argued at length before the Select Committee on Procedure during the last session of Parliament,[2] but met with determined Treasury opposition.

A similar attitude of resistance to any kind of standing parliamentary committee to inquire into taxation or tax proposals has been adopted by Treasury ministers and officials since the present Conservative Government assumed office. The only mitigating events have been Mr Barber's decisions to publish

2. *Second Special Report*, 302, HMSO, 27 May 1970.

Green Papers on value-added taxes and the reform of the corporation tax. The Select Committee on Procedure continues to press its demand for a sub-committee on taxation and finance to be formed by the recently established Select Committee on Expenditure.

Sir Richard Clarke, writing with the authority and knowledge of his long experience as a senior Treasury official, makes a powerful plea for a long-term, publicly announced taxation policy. He sees no reason why governments should not announce their intentions several years ahead, excluding of course the actual rates of taxation to be imposed; and this is precisely what Mr Barber has done in regard to value-added tax and promises to do in regard to corporation tax. Sir Richard deplores the mystique which has in the past surrounded the Chancellor's handling of taxation questions, producing what he calls the 'circus' atmosphere on Budget Day, in which the conjurer produces surprises and shocks for his audience by a wave of his magic wand. What is needed is a readiness on the part of government to consider expenditure and taxation together throughout their tenure of office, instead of giving priority to policies and decisions involving expenditure with the consequences in terms of taxation coming into the picture at a very much later date, and even then being regarded as the special prerogative of the Chancellor rather than as the responsibility of the government as a whole. If governments behaved in the manner advocated by Sir Richard this would give the greatest opportunity for discussion in Parliament and among the public. It is on such matters, too, that select committees of the House of Commons, Green Papers, and consultation with professional associations are likely to prove most fruitful.

It is painfully clear that successive post-war governments have not succeeded in solving, or helping to solve, our main economic problems by fiscal measures, and that they therefore need help from any quarter which can give it. The most obvious source is the House of Commons, working through a select committee staffed with experts. There is also a clear need for much more empirical research on the economic and social effects of taxes.

There is also the question of the administrative efficiency of our system of taxation. The Inland Revenue has in the past been one of the better departments of the British Government, which had acquired a reputation for courtesy, efficiency and integrity. But during recent years it has been overwhelmed by the huge additional tasks thrust upon it by capital-gains tax, corporation tax, and the fantastic complexities in the law introduced to counteract the devices for avoiding taxes and death duties by the army of professional advisers of the wealthy. This army includes many former Inspectors of Taxes who have left the Civil Service to become highly-paid consultants, thereby adding to the burden on those who remain. There are unmistakable signs that the work of the Inland Revenue has become much slower, much less accurate, and generally less efficient, partly because of the removal of offices from London to remote provincial towns, which makes personal calls by tax-payers impracticable, and also because of a great deal of mechanization and computerization, with all the defects which those labour-saving expedients have led us to expect in our dealings with shops and public utility undertakings.

Professor Wheatcroft[3] has declared that our progressive system of income tax is the most complicated in the world, with its different rules for assessing income tax and surtax, its distinction between earned and unearned income, its different reliefs and allowances, its different methods of treating the income of wives in relation to that of their husbands, etc. The present Government's decision to abolish short-term capital-gains tax and surtax will help to relieve the burden of administration, but much more is needed, especially in view of the impending introduction of value-added tax, which will place heavy additional burdens on the customs and excise. This again is a matter for immediate inquiry and here too a select committee would help; but some far larger and long-term inquiries must also take place: basic objectives need clarifying and, even if clarified, the knowledge is at present simply not there to predict the probable results of major changes in taxation policy.

3. 'A Study in Surtax', *The Banker*, March 1967, p. 206.

Professor Clayton and Mr Houghton stress the need for flexibility and the avoidance of complexity in the system of taxation. Complexity is the enemy of flexibility and is therefore to be discouraged whenever possible. It is obvious that simplification goes hand in hand with ease of administration, while complexity adds immensely to the burden falling on the Revenue Department, as well as on the citizen, on companies and their advisers, and on non-governmental organizations of many kinds.

Finally, we come to value-added taxation. Here we move from the present to the future and, so far as this country is concerned, from the known to the unknown. Possibly some of the anti-marketeers will soon be singing the praises of our dear old British purchase tax and explaining that selective employment tax fitted the unique characteristics of the nation in a way no new-fangled foreign importation could do. Mr Stout points out that the principal advantages of value-added tax over these taxes lie in its neutrality, and in the absence of spill-over into exports, capital investment, or business costs. VAT, unlike purchase tax, does not discriminate in favour of grand pianos and yachts or against motorcars and bicycles. It is also neutral as regards different methods of production and distribution. Several important classes of goods and services will be exempted, but the general non-selectivity of VAT will be a substantial move towards bringing costs and prices closer together than they are at present. Large differences in the rates of VAT in different countries are, however, likely to continue indefinitely. And our specific duties on alcoholic liquor, cigarettes and tobacco will almost certainly remain.

Mr Stout has much to say about the desirable balance between direct and indirect taxation. What is chiefly interesting in his analysis is the extreme difficulty of forecasting where the ultimate burden of indirect taxes will fall, for this will depend on a number of factors outside the fiscal field. He states that the fiscal incidence of a tax change is determined by the circumstances in which it is introduced. One wonders whether in the present state of knowledge these can be sufficiently disentangled to trace the effects of a tax even retrospectively.

If VAT were opposed on the ground that it is regressive, it would be possible to rectify this by means of a system of *per capita* consumption allowances. Mr Stout is of the opinion that our present system of indirect taxation, taken as a whole, is regressive; that its regressiveness offsets the progressiveness of our direct taxes over a wide range of incomes; and that it is through the distribution of benefits through the social services that redistribution of resources takes place and not through the system of taxation.

But how certain is it that even the direct taxes are progressive? Sir Richard Clarke states that below the upper 2 per cent of personal incomes taxation is broadly proportionate to income – which means that it is not progressive at all except for a very small minority in receipt of very large incomes. He writes that it is by reason of the larger share of social security benefits which the lower-income groups receive that the total effect of state action is progressive. But note the narrowness of this reference to social security benefits. If we were to look at education or the health service it is doubtful if a similar conclusion could be drawn in respect of those services.

Considerations such as these lead to the conclusion that the time is ripe for the appointment of a Royal Commission on the causes of poverty; for, despite all our efforts to create and maintain a welfare state, a substantial amount of poverty still exists. That this is partly due to the system of taxation can no longer be doubted.

2
Cuts in Government Spending and the Tax Illusion

SAMUEL BRITTAN*

This essay is concerned with the thesis that governments should look for cuts in public expenditure – or strictly speaking in its planned growth – to make room for reductions in personal taxation. It is not concerned with the question of whether the tax cuts should be larger or smaller than the public expenditure cuts to give the economy at any given time a stimulus or a check. The first is a highly political question involving the allocation of resources. The second is a question of demand management which belongs to a different realm of discourse; and nothing but confusion can come from lumping the two together.

The general argument I want to put across is that the tax philosophy with which the Conservatives came to power in 1970 was based on a fairly primitive confusion to which I shall give the label 'tax illusion'. This does not prevent many of the individual changes from being highly desirable. But the basic philosophy was muddled; and this muddle helps to explain the presence of some extremely undesirable changes, such as the new agricultural policy, and the false urgency attached to other measures which are being pushed through at an unsuitable time.

Such a critique may be of some interest, as the standpoint from which it is written includes a strong belief in the maximum freedom of personal choice and in returning to the individual

* The author writes in the *Financial Times*. He was formerly economic editor of the *Observer* and an adviser at the Department of Economic Affairs. His books include *Left or Right: The Bogus Dilemma* and *The Price of Economic Freedom*. This article draws on the new material in Chapters 3 and 11 of the final Penguin edition of *Steering the Economy*, published in 1971. Readers are referred to this volume for the wider economic, political and historical background.

many decisions now left to the public authorities. This standpoint involves a strong bias in favour of a market economy, and the view that, even where state intervention is necessary, the profit motive and price mechanism should be used as policy instruments in preference to administrative controls or public ownership. It is a standpoint which would be labelled by Labour Party traditionalists and by the bulk of political commentators as 'right wing', whether correctly or not.

Current Fallacies

What is to be gained from curbing public expenditure? 'Tax cuts' is too glib and superficial an answer. People are interested in the real value of their post-tax disposable incomes. Tax rates are only one element here. Pre-tax income and the level of prices are just as important elements in the picture. Any assessment of public expenditure cuts which stops short at the tax consequences and does not look at their other consequences is seriously misleading, even from the point of view of the most convinced believer in transferring spending power from the state to the individual.

The most flagrant example of a supposed public expenditure cut, which leaves citizens no better off, is the new agricultural policy which the Government decided to introduce irrespective of the outcome of the EEC negotiations. The 'savings' arising from switching from deficiency payments to levies are entirely spurious. The citizen pays less as tax-payer, and instead pays more for food in the shops. Indeed the change is worse than neutral. For so long as farm support is a charge on the budget there is at least some check on its size. Once it becomes just one of many items determining the cost of living, it is much more difficult to keep under control. While a change to levies may be a necessary evil as part of the bargain for EEC entry, to argue for the change independently is an example of the triumph of naïve budgetary arithmetic over the most elementary economics. Indeed we have had the ludicrous example of the Minister of Agriculture (before the transition to levies was complete) pleading with foreign suppliers to raise their prices and thus to worsen

British terms of trade and real incomes, because his Government was so blinded by the spurious budgetary saving that it could not see the real income loss involved.

A more harmless example is the switch from investment grants to more generous depreciation allowances and lower corporation tax. This is a trivial accountancy change. Very much the same amounts will be distributed to companies as before. Yet it appears in the figures as a very large saving in public expenditure.

Economists are often tempted to identify true public expenditure curbs, which *do* increase the real incomes available to citizens, with reductions in public spending on *goods and services* – weapons, armies, teachers' salaries, school-building, hospital services, and so on; and they are inclined to identify the spurious element with transfers and charges. The latter simply represent ways in which public expenditure can be financed, or ways of redistributing income, and do not affect the amount of spending power which can be left in individual hands.

This, alas, is an oversimplification. We can see this by examining the case of health service charges. So long as these are small and unrelated to the price of appliances, drugs or treatment, they can be looked upon as a tax, alternative to other taxes. But let us suppose that charges were to be closely related to the costs of particular treatment, and aimed to recover a high proportion of these costs. In the extreme case the state would be selling medical treatment at market prices and would be competing on equal terms with private suppliers. Medical treatment would have moved from the realm of collective to individual purchase and would have become like an industry in which state-owned firms competed with private firms. I am not arguing that anything going as far as this is likely. Indeed the moves originally planned in this direction have run into trouble. The point is simply that the balance between collective and private consumption can be changed by raising charges as well as by altering public expenditure on goods and services.

Another example relates to transfers. The new housing policy will raise council rents nearer to market levels; and there will be a rebate system extended to the private sector and tied strictly to income and needs. The net reduction in public expenditure on housing will reflect a reduction in the social service element in housing, and an increase in personal disposable incomes out of which people will have to make provision for their own accommodation.

Those of us who welcome changes of this kind should be careful not to exaggerate their magnitude. It is naïve in the extreme to equate real income gains with the crude tax savings. Let us take a skilled worker, who is deprived of a subsidy on a council house for which he now has to pay an economic rent and receives a tax cut in return. Let us assume too that the whole transaction amounts to £100 and that he breaks even arithmetically. He is nevertheless in a real sense better off, as he can now choose whether to spend the £100 to stay in the same house, to help finance alternative accommodation, or for some entirely different purpose. Equally, however, it is absurd to regard the gain in his real income as anything approaching £100.

If one looks at possible public expenditure cuts, there is a spectrum between two extremes. At one extreme come reductions in public expenditure which increase real incomes, via tax cuts, with no offset. The much-desired 'elimination of waste' or 'improvement in efficiency' is the paradigm example. A little further along the spectrum come defence cuts. There may be an offset in reduced security; but this is controversial, perhaps long delayed, and not obvious in the daily life of the citizen. In the middle come reductions in public spending which do increase the real value of people's take-home pay via tax reductions, but which also reduce the value of government services. Whether these are worth making or not is a matter of political judgement (which ought not to prevent the matter from being rationally discussed). At the other extreme are spurious budgetary savings, such as in investment grants or farm support, which correspond to no reduction in governmental activities (either in investment subsidy or in the transfer of incomes to farmers) and no increase in personal freedom of choice. They involve simply a change in mechanics, so that the exaction from the citizen is no longer called 'tax'.

As all this is rather abstract, it might be useful to illustrate it by looking at the changes made in the autumn and winter of 1970–71 by the newly elected Conservative Government in the public expenditure programme they inherited. The changes are shown for 1974–5, the latest available year, when the new policies would have had long enough to show their effects. The figures cover all cash outlays on the Treasury definition, including transfers and charges and net purchases of existing assets, as well as purchases of goods and services. If Labour had won the election it might also have made some changes – a summer stock-taking is normal when ministers receive the annual Public Expenditure Survey Committee (PESC) report. The following table is intended simply as a guide to the policies of the new Government. The one change made from the official table is that the £600 million savings on investment grants, which were to be balanced by a £590 million revenue loss on higher capital allowances and reduced corporation tax, have been omitted.[1]

The £156 million of agricultural and £132 million of defence cuts come at opposite ends of the spectrum discussed above. The agricultural 'cuts' are simply a way of disguising the same overall farm burden. On the other hand, the defence cuts will in principle leave more available, pound for pound, for the ordinary citizen – although I am not competent to judge the security trade-off, or the controversy about whether the original figures really represented the Labour Government's actual intentions.

The £115 million of cuts in health and education are more than accounted for by increased charges of various kinds, and the ending of cheap welfare and school milk for most pupils. Thus they could be added to the housing 'cuts' which represent mainly higher council rents. We then have a total of £265 million which represents a shift towards charging market prices for services provided by the state. Those who prefer individuals to be given a free choice in spending their incomes and state help to be provided in cash will welcome these changes, provided the effects on the distribution of income are acceptable (of which

1. As a result of the second corporation-tax cut in April 1971, the state now loses on balance on the deal.

Table 1 Projected Public Expenditure in 1974–5
Changes made by Conservative Government

	£m (1970 Survey prices)
Agricultural price guarantees, etc.	−156
Housing	−150
Defence	−132
'Technology and industry' (excluding investment grants)	−117
Capital expenditure of nationalized industries	− 82
Education	− 59
Health	− 46
Transport and road	− 58
Miscellaneous local services	− 10
Research councils	− 5
Miscellaneous	− 2
	−817

Source: Table A7, pp. 68–9, *Public Expenditure 1969–70 to 1974–5*; Cmnd. 4578, 1971; Totals refer to 'policy changes', excluding abolition of investment grants.

more anon). But there is obviously a very clear offset to the resulting tax reductions; and the gain in real post-tax incomes is only a fraction of the nominal reductions; these items therefore come in the middle of the spectrum.

It is very difficult to say much in terms of general principle about the £82 million savings in the capital spending of state industries. To the extent that this is the elimination of waste, it corresponds to the 'genuine saving' end of the spectrum. To the extent that there is a reduction in the quality of service there is an offset. The absence of a fully competitive market for the industries concerned makes it difficult to draw a direct link between the profitability of the investment and the desire of consumers for its fruits.

The most interesting section is the £117 million saving on 'technology and industry' (excluding investment grants). When state aid for industrial projects or activity is withdrawn or reduced, the businessmen affected can react in three ways, or in some way intermediate between the alternatives:

1. They can withdraw from the activity.
2. They may finance it themselves out of profits.
3. They may finance it and pass the costs on to the consumer.

In the second case there will be a transfer of real income from certain firms to the rest of the community; and no switch from public to private consumption. In the third case we are again in the intermediate range of the spectrum. In contrast to agriculture, there is a genuine reduction in the degree of state support for the industries concerned (as there is nothing like an import levy system); but the gain in personal incomes via tax cuts is offset by price increases. In the first case, where the activities cease altogether, there is a clear public gain if all that is lost is the subsidization of prestige activities. But one must remember that buried in this item are a number of expenditures, such as the grant to the Consumer Council, which provide the information and research which make the market economy respond more sensitively to consumer needs. Similar objections apply to the withdrawal or threatened withdrawal of grants for commuter transport services. The unsubsidized prices of private road and public passenger transport do not reflect the true cost of these alternatives (because of congestion costs, etc.); and the withdrawal of support will actually impair the free exercise of consumer choice between correctly costed alternatives. But while the axes are falling in these socially and commercially desirable areas, Concorde and RB211 continue for prestige and make-work reasons and dwarf all the other economies in the industrial sector.

The Distribution of Income

So far the reader may have the impression that this essay has been discussing Hamlet without the Prince; and he would be right. The Labour Party has an instinctive desire for as much public expenditure as it can get away with, and the Conservative Party for as little as it can manage. The reason for this difference does not in fact turn on public expenditure itself, but on the distribution of income; and public expenditure is at the centre of the argument mainly because of its distributional implications. This has been explained by Brian Barry in a most important and insufficiently discussed book, *Political Argument*.[2] Under a British-type tax and benefit system, the higher the total tax burden, the more 'equal' is the post-tax distribution of income. For this reason egalitarians press for a high level of state spending, even if they are not collectivists. Non-egalitarians, on the other hand – in practice the middle classes and better-paid workers – feel bound to press for lower state-spending even if they would otherwise be enthusiastic about a high level of public services.

By a careful study of the incidence of total spending on different income and family circumstances, it would be possible to construct a system of direct and indirect taxes which would be distributionally neutral. (The tax system would have to compensate for the bias of the public expenditure system and therefore in itself be regressive.) If it were raised or lowered by x per cent and the proceeds distributed to or taken away from all public expenditure programmes on a *pro rata* basis, the allocation of post-tax income between income classes would remain unchanged. On top of this, there could be a special 'transfer fund' which would pay out cash benefits at the bottom end, and impose some form of progressive levy on income or capital at the upper end. The transfer fund need not be self-balancing and could if desired be fed from the main tax fund. But there would be a presumption that any increase in the rate of growth of public spending on goods and services would be paid for out of general

2. *Political Argument*, Routledge & Kegan Paul, 1965, pp. 156–7.

revenue, and that any reduction in such spending would accrue to the Treasury for the purpose of tax cuts. In this way the argument about equality and income distribution could be separated from that over public versus private spending.

The idea is quite feasible technically. The Treasury has already separated off a National Loans Fund (which covers net central government lending to other bodies) from the main 'Consolidated Fund', and a redistribution fund would be a separation of a similar kind. The obstacle does not lie in any administrative complications, but very much deeper. The last thing politicians want is a published fund, which makes it clear how much is redistributed from whom to whom. The net recipients would want still more and the net losers would be bitterly resentful at making even the existing transfer. Both left and right feel it safer to blur the question of how much would be redistributed to whom in a debate conducted on the basis of 'schools, houses and pensions' versus 'tax cuts and incentives'.

The Effects of Conservative Policy

Chancellors have a natural tendency to escape from their dilemmas by looking for a philosopher's stone. Every politician would like to find tax reforms which would make most people better off and no one worse off. In opposition, or in the early stages of government, they hope to do this by major changes in the whole tax and public expenditure system. Chancellors of established governments hope to do the same by ingenious manipulation of individual tax rates. Unfortunately the philosopher's stone for which they are looking does not exist. It is not possible to create resources out of thin air. Tax handouts may be given in some years in the supposed interest of demand management, just as taxes may be increased in other years for this reason. But it is an elementary error to confuse short-term cyclical variations with a long-term tax strategy.

The hard fact is that it is only at the top and at the bottom of the income range that major improvements can readily be made in real disposable incomes, because of the small numbers involved. For the vast majority of the tax-payers, who provide most of the revenue, only a limited amount can be done except through optical illusion. What matters to people's living standards is real personal disposable income after tax, and the real value of public services received in kind. It is all too easy to think up big switches in the public expenditure and tax system, involving hundreds of millions of pounds of nominal reductions, which, after vast administrative upheaval and bitter political wrangles, leave these key variables unaffected or lead only to small net changes in the distribution of incomes, which could more easily be made directly.

A calculation of the exact redistribution resulting from Conservative tax and public expenditure 'cuts' in their first year of office is complicated by the fact that the tax cuts exceeded the public expenditure cuts, since the Chancellor was trying to apply a stimulus to the economy. Therefore it seemed as if everybody had benefited. One has to guess what would have happened in a normal year, when either the tax cuts would have been limited to the public spending curbs, or the latter would have had to be made more severe. A full calculation would also take into account those changes which simply offset the automatic effects of rapid inflation on a progressive tax system, which is particularly adverse at the lower and upper ends of the scale.

Allowing for this complication as best one can, it looks as if the Conservatives have redistributed income to both the lowest and upper (i.e. surtax) income groups by means of the family income supplement, higher child allowances, the increased graduation of national insurance contributions and the income and surtax cuts. The net amounts involved are fairly limited although important to the groups concerned. It would have been possible and desirable, as Mr Harold Lever suggested in the 1971 Finance Bill debate, to have financed the surtax reliefs by a reallocation of taxes among the better-off. Owing to the voluntary nature of the estate duties and the much lower rates of capital-gains tax, those with large wealth, or who can take their earnings in the form of capital gains, are taxed very lightly or not at all; while up to 1971 those whose earnings came as declared income and who were not good at avoidance techniques paid at confiscatory rates, which at the top approached 90 per cent; and as a result of inflation the very high rates were creeping down the income scale.

Even after the 1971 budget the UK had a top marginal direct tax rate of 75 per cent compared with 50–60 per cent in the USA and Germany. If the Conservative ministers had had the political courage and imagination to introduce a gifts and inheritance tax system and a moderate wealth tax, they could have gone down to the US and German rates of top marginal direct tax, and totally abolished the tax differential on unearned income (which is a penalty on risky investment) without any net cost to tax-payers in the lower ranges. As it is, it will not take too long for inflation to erode the recent surtax concessions, as it did those of Thorneycroft in 1957 and Selwyn Lloyd in 1961.

Apart from the help given at the top and the bottom, there has been a much more questionable shift within the middle income groups, as can be seen from the following table.

Table 2   Net Effect of Tax Reductions, Higher Charges and Exemptions, National Insurance Scheme Contributions and Family Income Supplement, April 1971

Family of 2 children (not over 11 years)

Annual income	*Net gain*
£780	+ 104
£1,040	+ 34
£1,300	+ 19
£1,560	+ 20
£2,080	+ 7
£2,500	+ 16
£3,000	+ 25
£4,000	+ 44
£5,000	+ 83

Source: Hansard, 5 April 1971. Extended up the income range with the aid of the *Financial Statement*.

The absolute figures are very misleading for several reasons: some of the supposed gains simply offset the automatic increase in the tax bills that would otherwise arise from inflation; the higher food prices resulting from the policy changes are excluded; and the element of general economic stimulus, which has nothing to do with the public expenditure package, may have to be reversed. Some of the people in the middle would therefore either break even or lose on a true calculation; but the *relative* effects are stated reasonably fairly. There is clearly a modest transfer from the £1,300–£3,000 a year bracket to the £3,000–£5,000 group. (As mentioned already, those above £5,000 gain much more individually – at least before allowing for inflation; but the total cost to other tax-payers is much smaller.) This transfer in question results mainly from the devotion of £350 million of the total available relief to a 2½-per-cent cut in the 'standard rate' for 1971–2. The gain or loss within the middle income band is very modest, both as a proportion of disposable income and of tax rates. The net sums in the table are the result of larger offsetting flows in both directions. The justification for the whole exercise is the supposed incentive effects of the income-tax reductions.

The reality or otherwise of the disincentive effects of high direct taxation is one of the most fiercely disputed economic issues between right and left. This argument is possible because taxes (whether direct or indirect) have a 'substitution' and an 'income' effect which point in different directions. The 'substitution' effect increases the attraction of leisure over work (and of undemanding work over demanding, but better-paid, work), the higher the rate of tax. On the other hand, the 'income effect' means that people have to work harder to obtain a given income, the higher the rate of tax. The net result can be in either direction.

But this is not a reason for complete agnosticism. The 'substitution' effect relates to marginal tax rates, the 'income' effect to the average rate paid by the tax-payer on his whole income (the Inland Revenue calls this the 'effective' rate). The fierce resistance of many left-inclined economists to the 'incentive argument' is probably justified in the case of the standard rate cut for the ordinary income-tax payer; but the 'incentive argument' is much more likely to be right for the upper income group. In the £3,000–£5,000 a year bracket (which gains more from the income-tax cut than it loses from the other changes), the pre-1971 marginal rate of 32 per cent was not all that different from the 'effective' rate of around 25 per cent; and it is quite possible that the 'income' effect was as large as, or larger than, the 'substitution' effect. Above £6,000, however, marginal rates ranged from 50 to 90 per cent, whereas the average or effective rate on the whole of a person's income was under 30 per cent at £6,000 and only just over 50 per cent at £15,000. Thus the tax system did very much less to reduce the total value of higher incomes than it did to discourage extra effort at the margin.

Even if one were unsure about the effects of surtax changes, they could have been costless in the way advocated above; and even the way the Chancellor did finance them was trivial in cost (£38 million[3] or well under 0.1 per cent of the Gross National Product). There was nothing to be lost from taking a chance on the incentive effect and cutting drastically the more penal marginal rates, except from the point of view of those who derive a positive utility from the discomfiture of the better-paid. There was in any case no justification for singling out income for specially severe treatment, when – despite nominally high rates of estate duty – large property owners were and are much more lightly treated; and it is in the distribution of property, rather than earned income, that the most glaring inequalities are to be found.

My main aim, however, is not to impose these distributional judgements on the reader, but to show that such judgements could, if we wished, be separated from discussions of public expenditure. All the elements in the Government's public expenditure package, including the reduction in school meal subsidies and higher health service charges, could have been achieved without the adverse relative effect on lower-middle-

3. The cut remains trivial even if we add the £2 million for the option of separation for a wife's earnings and the disaggregation of a child's investment income.

income families. This could have been done through a different pattern of tax reduction – for instance through higher personal tax-allowances and bigger income-related social security benefits.[4] Looking at it from the Conservative point of view, the Government could have made all the changes it wanted in relative post-tax incomes by directly adjusting the tax progression, without having swung the axe over everything that was statistically classified as public expenditure.

Wages and Prices

Quite apart from the intrinsic merits of the Conservative public expenditure package, one must bear in mind its effects on the cost of living – and therefore on inflationary expectations – at a time when wage inflation was our Number One economic problem. The public expenditure measures (including the effects of the farm price review) were likely to add about 1 per cent to retail prices in 1971–2 and about 3 per cent by 1974–5. By comparison, the halving of selective employment tax in 1971 may reduce the index by about $\frac{1}{2}$ per cent.

Faced with the difficulty of making many more cuts in public expenditure, the Government may be tempted to pitch the value-added tax at a rate high enough to finance further income-tax cuts. Even if it does not do this, any attempt to recover from value-added tax any net increase which may be required in total tax revenue will raise the price index further. (If there were any reduction in indirect taxes by means of the regulator for anti-recession reasons, this would almost certainly have either to be reversed at a later date or recovered from other taxes.)

Admittedly, a given tax burden appears to be resented less if it is paid indirectly through higher prices in the shops than if it is

4. This essay, in common with nearly all similar studies, is based on the false assumption that there is no shifting forward of direct taxes to pre-tax earnings. This is certainly false; but the degree of shifting is unknown. So long as the state has *some* power to affect the distribution of post-tax income, the statistical calculations give an idea of direction, although they exaggerate the amounts involved.

levied directly on incomes. There would in normal circumstances be something to be said for respecting this illusion of the public and making a net shift from direct to indirect taxes. Great caution should, however, be exercised about making such a shift in the early 1970s when, quite apart from the unprecedentedly high level of wage settlements, there are numerous other forces liable to raise costs and prices, and thereby give wage inflation itself an upward push. These include equal pay and the effects on food prices of the new Conservative farm policy and other policies, not to speak of the Common Market agricultural policy. To add to these forces by gratuitously pushing up indirect taxes would be sheer folly.

What Should be Provided Collectively?

Enough has been said to show that the Conservative *penchant* for hacking away (not always very successfully) at the list of items known as public expenditure, and the Labour tendency (at least in opposition) to fight to the death to preserve all the threatened items, are not the most sensible ways of conducting our affairs. The outsider can only hope that the items cut by one government will not be identical with those increased by another, and that the alternation of governments and parties will lead to some net improvement in the mix.

What would then be a better criterion to adopt? I have already argued the case for treating redistribution of income separately from public expenditure. We are then left with the fundamental question of which goods and services we wish to purchase collectively rather than privately.

The concept of a 'public good' is of help in answering it. In the case of a pure public good one person's enjoyment does not diminish the amount available for others; and if it is provided at all, it is impossible to limit access by a charging system. Pure public goods would include national defence or clean air. An example of a pure private good would be a refrigerator or a meal. In between the two extremes there is a big intermediate category such as medical services, education or slum clearance, which are not pure public goods, but which have semi-public aspects. The demolition of slums has large 'spill-over' effects on the general appearance of the city, which all can enjoy. Except for a few motorways, it would be difficult to organize a charging system for new roads; and until a certain degree of utilization is reached, one person's enjoyment does not detract from another's.[5]

The main controversies relate to this area of semi-public goods. In practice there are many gradations in the extent to which goods are purchased collectively or privately. In the extreme case of defence, the purchase is collective; it is provided 'free' to the citizen and private provision is forbidden. One stage further are services where private provision is permissible, but the collective variety comes without charge and thus tends to become the norm for the majority of the population. Schools are a case in point. Further along the line come collectively purchased services, for which a charge is made, but at less than full cost – parts of the health service being an obvious example.

The question of state ownership should be strictly separated from that of collective versus private purchase. If the state electricity undertakings provided electricity along commercial lines, this would in no way reduce the proportion of the national incomes available for private citizens to dispose of as they wish. Conversely, if schools and hospitals were privately owned, but the state paid all the bills, their services would be collectively purchased; and the tax contributions required to finance these state purchases would be a deduction from the freely disposable income of citizens.

It is thus possible to draw two axes showing the extent to which services are in the public sector. In one quadrant are the armed services, whose products are collectively purchased and provided by public authorities (there are no private armies, although one might argue about security services and guard dogs). In the opposite quadrant are refrigerators, privately purchased

5. For an excellent discussion of private and public goods, see Charles L. Schultze, *The Politics and Economics of Public Spending*, Brookings Institute, Washington, 1968.

from private manufacturers. One mixed category contains electricity (considered as a final output), publicly provided, but privately purchased. In another mixed category come weapons of defence, made by private firms, but collectively purchased. There are of course numerous intermediate categories, from education in schools to psychoanalysis and travel agencies, where there is a mixture of collective and private activity, both in provision and in purchase.

The Treasury definition of public expenditure – while useful for the control purpose for which it was devised – is based on a confusing mixture of ownership and purchase. All collective purchases are included; the investment of all state undertakings is included, but not their current sales. The purchase of existing undertakings by the state counts as public expenditure; denationalization or 'hiving off' is negative expenditure. This concept of public expenditure encourages the myth that the selling off of state assets would allow taxes to be reduced. It does no such thing. The demand placed on the economy by the investment expenditure of the British Steel Corporation or Thomas Cook is not reduced if their boards borrow directly from the market instead of the Treasury borrowing for them. It is true that the lower government-borrowing requirement will tend to reduce the growth of money supply, but an equivalent effect could – if desired – be achieved by open market operations and/or the use of Special Deposits. There are some arguments for 'hiving off'; but reducing tax and raising personal disposable income is not one of them. The Treasury is, of course, aware of this; and in its own budget recommendations would not dream of allowing any tax concessions as a result of 'hiving off'.

The question of the proportion of economic activity under state ownership or control should be settled by entirely different criteria from those governing collective expenditure. The relevant issues for the former are in my view the desirability of encouraging competition, and the effect on personal liberty if the state share is too large. The public sector comprises about 24 per cent of the nation's manpower (public administration and services, 16 per cent, the nationalized industries, 8 per cent) and 60 per cent of these with full-time higher education. As John Stuart Mill put it in *On Liberty*:

> If the roads, the railways, the banks, the insurance offices, the great joint-stock companies, the universities, and the public charities, were all of them branches of the government; if, in addition, the municipal corporation and local boards, with all that now devolves on them, became departments of the central administration; if the employés of all these different enterprises were appointed and paid by the government, and looked to the government for every rise in life; not all the freedom of the press and popular constitution of the legislature would make this or any other country free, otherwise than in name.

My own judgement would be that we have not yet passed the danger point for liberty, although we have at times been pretty close to it, especially in the sphere of employment for those with higher education. A fuller analysis of the problem would have to pay careful attention, on Mill's lines, to the degree of independence of government of other parts of the public sector, such as the nationalized industries and local authorities.

The debate on public expenditure should not revolve around these questions, but on the choice between collective and private purchases of different goods and services. This has to be discussed sector by sector and I cannot embark on it here.[6] To my mind, it is a question of balancing the advantages of personal choice against the economies of collective purchases and provision (e.g. parks in cities) and any other spill-over gains there may be in the state method. There are so-called 'integrationists' who attach great value to making sure all citizens have the same kind of medical treatment, schooling, etc. This involves a belief not merely in equality but in uniformity and would not be taken into account by anyone who puts a high value on individual choice.

Having decided what goods and services should be treated as public or semi-public goods, we should then decide how much to spend on them. There is no necessary connection between views

6. I have discussed it to a small extent in *Government and the Market Economy*, Institute of Economic Affairs, 1971.

on the services which ought to be supplied collectively and views on the amount that ought to be spent on them once this decision has been made. There is no inconsistency in believing that insufficient is spent on the vast range of goods and services for which the state has, at present, a near monopoly of purchase, but that some of these services should, in an affluent society, be treated as private goods and left to individuals of average incomes and above to provide from their own resources.

APPENDIX:
THE DEFINITION OF PUBLIC EXPENDITURE

The defects in the approach of governments and oppositions to public expenditure are encouraged by the way in which public expenditure is defined and measured. I have tried to avoid discussion of definitions in the main article, but the subject cannot be dodged altogether. There exists in fact a bewildering variety of alternative definitions of public expenditure. The differences between them are far from being minor technicalities. Nonpartisan estimates of public expenditures given for different purposes in official publications range from about 20 per cent of the Gross National Product to well over 50 per cent.

The definition of public expenditure most widely used for planning purposes in Whitehall is not surprisingly one that is known as *the Treasury definition*. It is much the widest of definitions in common currency. It covers the whole of the current and capital expenditure of central and local government on goods and services and transfers, the gross outgoings of the national insurance funds, and the capital spending of nationalized industries. It is the most comprehensive of the definitions and is quite independent of parliamentary formalities. Defined in this way public expenditure amounted in 1970 to some 52–3 per cent of the GNP, and had risen from about 43 per cent in both 1959 and 1964.

The Treasury definition is a helpful indicator of the flows of spending, which in some sense pass through public hands, and is, therefore, useful for control purposes. It is no part of my argument that figures based on this definition should be suppressed. Nevertheless its use on the standard definition provides an extremely misleading impression.

It is quite untrue that over 50 per cent of the National Product is taken in taxation; it is quite untrue that anything approaching

50 per cent of economic activity is under the control of the state; and the proportion of the national output purchased collectively by the public authorities, rather than by individuals or firms, is nothing like 50 per cent. There is no point in the Treasury replying that public expenditure, defined in this way, ought not to be taken as a percentage of the GNP and invested with a political or social meaning. If any one set of figures is regarded as *the* standard definition, it is bound to be compared with some measures of national output.

Nor is it only the innocent layman, minister or MP who falls into this trap. Sir Samuel Goldman, the Second Permanent Secretary in the Treasury in charge of this area, told the Commons Public Expenditure General Sub-Committee: 'The proportion of the total GNP taken by public expenditure is pretty well known. It is of the order of 50 per cent or a little more.'[7] This is misleading in most of the ways in which the words were likely to be understood by his hearers or members of the public. Not merely does the official definition fail to answer basic questions about the division of national expenditure between private and collective spending; it does not give a good idea even of the crude tax-burden resulting from the expenditure of the public authorities. The Treasury definition overstates the burden on the citizen by leaving out sources of revenue other than taxes, of which the most important are the gross trading surpluses of the nationalized industries, and the next most important are local authority rents.

The extent of this exaggeration can be shown by Table 3 (overleaf) for a recent year.

The burden imposed on the population by public expenditure amounted in 1968–9 to £15,700 million or some 42½ per cent of the GNP. This is a good deal less than the impression given by the Treasury definition before deductions.

Why do we want a definition of public expenditure at all? The following are among the many possible reasons:

1. For overall purposes of Treasury control.

7. Minutes of Evidence, 29 March 1971.

2. To forecast or analyse the total demand on the economy now or in future years as an aid to overall economic strategy.
3. To discover the share of resources devoted to collective rather than public purchases.
4. As an index of the proportion of economic activity that is in some sense under government direction.
5. To see how much is left for *spending out of income* after taxes, rates, national insurance contributions and similar exactions.

Table 3   The Burden of Public Expenditure 1968–9

		£m
Public expenditure, Treasury definition		19,150
Deduct:	£m	
1. Public sector trading surpluses	1,500	
2. Rents received	900	
3. Interest and dividend receipts	250	
4. Import deposits	350	
5. Miscellaneous	150	
6. Net borrowing requirement	300	
Total deductions		3,450
Total public expenditure to be financed from rates, taxes and national insurance contributions		15,700

Source: *National Income and Expenditure, 1969*, and *Financial Statement 1969–70* (figures rounded).

I would suggest that the fifth concept is the one that is not necessarily the most fundamental, but of the greatest general interest. It is what most people instinctively have in mind when they talk of public expenditure; and if there is to be one principal definition it should be related to this concept. It will be noted that transfers are included in it. For the ordinary family, a deduction to pay for pensions is just as much part of the burden of public expenditure as taxes to pay for defence or schools.

My tentative conclusion is that we should seize the bull by the horns and define a concept of the *burden of public expenditure*, identically equal to what people pay in rates, taxes, insurance contributions and other such deductions from income. For 1968–9, this would have been the £15,700 million figure shown in Table 3 above, or 42½ per cent of the GNP.

The concept I am putting forward suffers from at least two weaknesses. The first is that, as discussed in the main text, people are interested in the *real* value of their post-tax incomes; and a concept of public expenditure related to the tax burden will allow governments to show an apparent saving in public expenditure offset by an increase in prices – such as the switch from deficiency payments to levies – as a genuine saving. I have not been able to think of any definition which will prevent this occurring. It can only be prevented by politicians operating with more sophisticated objectives than simply axing or boosting public expenditure, according to their political colour; or, short of that, by an extremely vigilant parliamentary and public scrutiny of the real meaning of proclaimed changes in public expenditure.

A second difficulty is that while transfers to other people's families are a clear burden to the tax-payer, transfers to the tax-payer's own family are not. Family allowances, which offset part of the tax bill, are hardly a burden to those who receive them. This difficulty would be resolved if all taxes and receipts were commuted into a single payment – positive or negative (this is the negative or reverse income-tax idea). Without actually adopting a negative income tax, it might in principle be possible to take off from the proposed definition of the burden of public expenditure those cash receipts which simply offset tax for the particular families involved. If this figure were known, it would be easy to include it among the deductions.

A possible third objection, which I do not find so worrying, is that the tax burden resulting from a given amount of public expenditure depends on the savings ratio. A given total could be financed with less tax if the savings ratio were to rise. The deduction of the public-sector borrowing requirement in Table 3 in fact gets round this objection. For the behaviour of the savings ratio will be among the many influences affecting the amount of public expenditure which can safely be financed by borrowing. The public-sector borrowing requirement is a way of summarizing all the many economic influences other than gross public expenditures and non-tax receipts which affect the tax burden; and its inclusion is in my view a strength rather than a weakness of the suggested presentation. The burden of public expenditure *is* less in a year when more of it can be financed by borrowing; and this should be taken into account in the presentation.

The suggested concept is, of course, of the *burden* of public expenditure rather than public expenditure itself. This is perfectly acceptable; for my argument is that it is this burden that the principal definition should seek to show.

The proposed presentation also has the advantage of dodging the problem of whether the investment of state industries should be included. If such investment is offset by surpluses or by a larger permissible government borrowing requirement than would exist if the industries were in private hands, the appropriate deductions are made in the table and no net burden results. Nationalized investment only appears as part of the net burden of public expenditure if it gives rise to an extra call on the taxpayer. Similarly an act of denationalization, which appears in the official definition as disinvestment, but which does not reduce demand by a corresponding extent and does not permit an equivalent reduction of taxes, would be reflected in the table as a reduction in the permissible borrowing requirement; and the final figure of the burden of public expenditure would not be distorted.

Indeed, Table 3 could be extended to show the effects of changes in public spending and taxes in line with a wide variety of different views about 'what really matters'. For example, if the focus of interest is direct taxes, indirect taxes and all other sources of revenue can be included among the deductions; and – given the borrowing requirement – one could see the implications for direct tax of hypothetical changes in either public expenditure or alternative sources of revenue. The presentation also deals neatly with the question of charges. Those who feel that they are basically alternative forms of taxes, can add back charges to the line 'Public expenditure, Treasury definition' now given net of them. The bottom line will then read 'Public expenditure to be financed from rates, taxes, national insurance contributions and charges'. Reductions in, say, income tax, paid for by higher charges, will not then appear as a reduction in the burden of public expenditure. The table can be made as detailed as one likes; and not all charges would have to be treated in the same way. In other words, apart from providing one basic definition of the burden of public expenditure, the table would provide a systematic link between public expenditure and taxes, and a do-it-yourself kit for anyone to measure the burden of public expenditure in any way he thinks appropriate.

Most of the space in this appendix has been devoted to grappling with purpose 5 (page 42) of a definition of public expenditure. Definitions for some of the other purposes are easier to find. For 'Treasury control', it would be best to accept the official Treasury definition evolved for that purpose. For demand forecasting and analysis, the relevant division is between 'expenditure on resources' (i.e. goods and services) and transfers and purchases of existing assets, now given in the Public Expenditure White Papers.

A definition suited to the third purpose – the share of resources devoted to collective purchases – is much more difficult for the reasons given in the main text. It would be tempting to measure this by the figure of expenditure on goods and services just mentioned in connection with the economic definition, but given gross of charges. Measured in this way, it has been running at about 25 per cent of the GNP. But some transfers are tied to specific purchases – e.g. rent subsidies – and are in many ways more like collective provisions; while charges which are fairly high and related to cost have the effect of removing some of the collective element from the services purchased. To obtain a true figure for collective purchases, one should probably deduct charges, but add back all those transfers, including housing subsidies and investment grants, which are conditional on certain kinds of purchase by the recipients and not part of their freely disposable incomes. There is also a case for deducting the investment of the nationalized industries, which is closer in economic purpose to private investment than to investment in the public services.

The fourth purpose of a public expenditure definition, measuring the proportion of economic activity under state direction, can lead to endless controversy. But a simple approach is to say that the state has in some sense direct control over public-sector employment, which accounts for about 24 per cent of the total. One might also add in state purchases from the private sector, as these give the state great potential leverage over the supplying firms. Such purchases were running at £5,000 million in 1970, and gave the state indirect control over perhaps another 10 per cent of total employment, thus amounting to a grand total of around 34 per cent.

3
Taxation and Social Justice

D. D. RAPHAEL*

I have been asked to contribute to this symposium from the point of view of political philosophy. Let me begin with the general question: what is taxation for? First, to finance the working of government and the services it provides; but secondly, to contribute directly to some of the aims of government. Putting the two together, the simple general question 'What is taxation for?' can be given the simple general answer 'To enable government to do its job'. But what is its job? That is controversial, and that is where political philosophy comes in.

The first and fundamental job of government is not controversial. It is to maintain order and security. For that purpose a government must organize and pay for a legal system with police and penal services, a defence force, and an administrative service. Two or three centuries ago this would have been quite enough for an old-style 'liberal' political theorist, someone like John Locke, for instance. The task of government was to protect the life, liberty, and property of its citizens. Its function was negative, to preserve the *status quo* of rights, leaving people as much freedom as possible, so long as they did not encroach on the freedom of others. This limitation of the job of government to protecting freedom was, in principle, continued by the utilitarian liberals of the nineteenth century. It lies behind John Stuart Mill's criterion for determining the boundary between individual liberty and social authority. But in practice the utilitarians, and especially J. S. Mill, assigned to government a wider function than the negative one of simply protecting freedom. They believed in *laissez-faire* economics, but in respect of social services they were taking the first steps to the welfare state.

* The author is Professor of Philosophy in the University of Reading.

The first and negative function of government, the maintenance of order and security, can be contrasted with a second and positive function, the promotion of welfare and justice. In speaking of the promotion of welfare I mean that government should actively encourage (with financial help) the growth of the economy and of public services, both material services such as hospitals, power supply, and communications, and non-material services like education, art galleries, and museums. In speaking of the promotion of justice I mean that government should go in for some redistribution of existing rights so as to make the pattern of rights more fair.

In a sense the first and negative function can also be said to promote, or at least to protect, welfare and justice. For if government protects a man's rights and stops other people from encroaching on them, then (*a*) it is protecting his interests or welfare, and (*b*) it is preventing injustice in safeguarding his rights. But the first function leaves it to a man's own efforts to increase his stock of welfare and the area of his rights. The second, positive, function makes it the job of government, representing collective responsibility, to add to the stock of welfare and to modify the existing distribution of rights.

All these functions of government affect its fiscal policy. Obviously the organizing of services costs money, whether these services are designed to protect existing rights or to increase people's welfare. Policies of encouraging economic growth and maintaining full employment require industrial incentives here and disincentives there. The redistribution of rights involves (though this is not the whole of the story) a redistribution of income and wealth. It is the last of these that brings up the issue of social justice.

All justice is social, in that justice always has to do with relationships between men, relationships within groups, be they small or large. There is no such thing as individual justice in the sense of something that concerns one individual alone, in isolation from everybody else. But when people talk about 'social justice' as if it were one kind of justice to be contrasted with another kind, I suppose they mean to contrast it with legal justice. The law defines and defends existing positive rights. These rights, legal rights, do not always strike us as morally justifiable, and they often fail to include things to which we should say a man had a moral right. The call for social justice is a call that legal rights should coincide with moral rights, that moral rights should be recognized and protected by law.

But there is more than one conception of moral rights. In particular there is a striking difference of opinion between people who base moral rights mainly on merit or desert, and those who add and emphasize the concepts of equality and need. Conservatives and right-wing liberals take the former view, socialists and radical liberals take the latter. You do not hear the first group talking very much about *social* justice; they will tell you that distribution according to merit is 'just', *tout court*. It is the advocates of equality and need who are fond of the label of *social* justice, so much so that the term 'social justice' comes close to meaning a socialistic conception of justice. Nevertheless, everyone in present-day Britain, whether he be socialist, liberal, or conservative, will make social justice one of his aims. He will agree that the state should act as if every citizen had an equal right to the satisfaction of at least basic needs. This is what the welfare state is all about, and nobody would want to scrap the welfare state altogether.

How much priority should social justice be given in taxation policy? There is no authoritative answer to that question. Everyone must answer it for himself as best he can. Political philosophy cannot answer the question; political philosophy cannot settle priorities. What political philosophy can do is to try to clarify the issues, so that individuals may be in a better position to form their own judgements about priorities.

Take for instance the general agreement that the welfare state is here to stay. One's idea of the welfare state can vary according to one's political sympathies. A socialist will say that everyone in need is entitled to the help of the community at large. So he may conclude that the right way to finance the social services is from general taxation graduated according to means. The rich should pay for the needs of the poor. It is a responsibility laid upon the rich by the claims of social justice. 'From each according to his ability, to each according to his needs.' A liberal, however, even a radical liberal (who, of course, is often likely to vote Labour), will think that is too simple. It is not enough to talk of the claims of need and the responsibilities of the wealthy to help the poor. What about the responsibility of every man to help himself? What about self-respect, the desire (the need, if you like) to be independent, not to depend on the charity of others? And so we find a liberal like Lord Beveridge building into the structure of the welfare state the semblance of payment by each man for his entitlement to benefit. Rich and poor alike pay the same weekly national insurance contribution. In fact, of course, that does not cover the cost of the benefits; a lot of it still has to come from general taxation. But if the working man pays what is for him quite a large sum each week, he will feel, when he is entitled to unemployment- or sickness-benefit, that he has paid for it, that he is not a recipient of charity. This is a concession to the idea of justice as based upon contract and desert. He is entitled to it, he has worked for it, he has paid for it, he deserves it. It is a *quid pro quo*; a return for what has been put in. 'From each according to his ability, to each according to his work.'

Here we have a difference of opinion about methods of financing certain social services. One way is to pay for them entirely from general taxation, which is graduated according to means. Another is to pay for them, at least in part, by a social insurance scheme with a flat rate of contribution for all, irrespective of means. A third method, which looks like a compromise, but is in principle a form of the first method, is the one used in the USA and New Zealand (and doubtless in other countries too). Social insurance contributions are separated from general taxation, but a man's contribution, subject to an upper limit, is dependent on means. He pays a small percentage of each dollar he earns, but with a ceiling that makes the maximum contribution fairly modest. The difference in these methods, and especially between the first and the second, reflects the contrast between two concepts of justice.

When we come to different views about taxation generally, the contrast is rather between justice and utility. An advocate of social justice will favour a steeply graduated scheme of income tax, and heavy death duties or inheritance tax in order to reduce inequalities, especially inequalities that owe nothing to merit. He may well talk about the needs of the poor for which the money can be used, but he is more likely to talk about reducing inequality. On the other side we hear of the disincentive effects of high taxation and high death duties; the argument (be it well or ill founded) is that a high rate of tax causes some people to work less hard than they might and so to produce less than they might for the wealth of the community as a whole.

The two concepts of justice that I described earlier can be accommodated under one general formula of distributive justice: in the distribution of benefits and burdens, differences must be justified by relevant differences in the recipients. Thus it is just to give more money to *A* than to *B*, if *A* is more deserving or if *A* is more needy; and it is just to give more responsibility to *C* (or to ask more of him) than *D*, if *C* is the more able to bear the responsibility or to make the contribution asked. In the absence of any such differences between *A* and *B* or *C* and *D*, it will be just to treat them equally. The general formula does not offer a way of settling conflicts in the interpretation of justice, because it does not spell out what is and what is not to count as a 'relevant' difference. Merit is relevant, need is relevant, ability is relevant; having a black skin or blue eyes or a captivating figure is not relevant. But the formula does not say why the one set of qualities is relevant and the other not. Nor does it say in what circumstances the requirements of justice apply and in what circumstances they do not. (For instance, if I give birthday presents to my blue-eyed lady friends, I am not being unjust when I favour them purely because I like their *beaux yeux*.) Nor again does the formula tell me how to grade priorities among the relevant qualities, whether to put merit above need or vice versa.

Still, taking the formula of distributive justice as a whole, how far does it conflict with social utility? There is no conflict between utility and the distribution of benefits according to merit, because this kind of distribution is itself useful. Take the examples of 'merit awards' in industry or among medical consultants. The merit award goes to the firm or the individual thought to be specially beneficial for the wealth or the health of the community; and the award is intended to act as an incentive, to the recipient and to others, to go on benefiting the community. A taxation policy which favours merit (such as useful talent or effort) contributes to general utility by giving incentives to people who are able to add to social benefit. Merit and utility go hand in hand. It is both just and useful to give incentives for work (or for short-term self-denial in the form of savings or investment) that benefits society.

So when people complain of the disincentive effect of high taxation, they can quite properly say that it is unjust as well as socially harmful. The man who works hard does not get the full reward of his labours when he is required to pay in taxes a larger proportion than usual of the extra money he earns. Whether or not this situation really acts as a disincentive I do not know. Professor Peston says in his article that there is no hard evidence that it does; but he also says that there is a very widespread belief that it does. Is there an equally widespread belief that a high tax on extra effort is unfair? I should guess not. And if that is correct, it is because the reward of merit is only one aspect of fairness or justice. Insofar as high taxation diminishes the reward of merit, it has an element of unfairness. But insofar as it is intended to apportion burdens according to ability to pay, or else to reduce inequality, it makes a positive contribution to fairness or justice.

The distribution of burdens or responsibilities in accordance with ability to bear them, like the distribution of benefits according to merit, does not conflict with social utility. When the responsibilities of carrying out functions are allotted, it is obviously going to be socially useful to give people the jobs that they can do well, and socially harmful to follow the opposite policy. The same is true of the distribution of financial burdens. The state is more likely to get the money it needs if it asks the rich, who can afford it, to pay more, and the poor to pay less. To ask everyone to pay an equal share, irrespective of means, would be inefficient as well as unfair.

A conflict between social utility and justice can arise, however, when we come to the elements of justice that the socialist and the radical emphasize: meeting needs and promoting equality. Meeting needs does not always go against social utility. Consider the example of a man of working age who is unemployed or sick. He needs unemployment- or sickness-benefit, and he needs the opportunity to find another job or the medical care to restore his health. It all costs money; social services, a full employment policy, and a health service. But obviously this is going to pay off; it is money well spent. The sooner the man can be back at work, the sooner will he be making his contribution to the national economy instead of being a drain on it. Sometimes, however, the meeting of needs brings no social return. Old-age pensions and geriatric services are not going to add anyone to the pool of active workers. Money spent on old people, or on the chronically sick, cannot be justified in terms of social utility. If a society were motivated purely by thought of social utility, it would say that money so spent is money wasted, and it would let its old people die, or perhaps even save more money by killing them and using their bodies for food. It is purely an idea of justice which says that the needs of the old and the chronically sick give them a right to social aid.

Nobody in a modern society would dream of querying the claim of justice against utility to meet such needs. Different people will have different opinions about the *degree* to which justice should outweigh social utility. Again the division coincides with that between the left and the right of the political spectrum. Socialists will favour raising pensions to provide a decent subsistence, even though this will mean higher taxes or other forms of contribution from people of working age. Conservatives will stress the disincentive effect of these measures and will conclude, with regret, that many of the elderly must put up with some hardship.

The same sort of split shows up more markedly when it comes to the redistribution of income or wealth purely for the sake of reducing inequality. Often such a policy is tied up with meeting needs, the needs of poverty. But even if you had a society with no real poverty, a socialist would still say that it is morally offensive to have a wide span between the extremes of wealth and relative poverty. Why does he say this?

A cynical explanation is that the feeling of moral offensiveness is the result of natural human envy. We should all like to have lots of money and the things that money can buy; and those who cannot afford champagne and a Rolls envy those who can. Envy turns into resentment, and resentment is expressed as a sense of injustice. That is the cynical explanation. Like most cynical views it is distorted by exaggeration. Adam Smith thought class distinction depends on the fact that the average man admires 'the rich and the great' because he takes sympathetic pleasure in the enjoyments which the rich can have and which we should all like to have. No doubt this is an exaggeration too, due to wearing rose-tinted spectacles; or perhaps we have become more sour in the twentieth century. Still, there is some truth in it, as there is in the story about envy.

While allowing that one element of the sense of justice arises from feelings such as resentment of harm inflicted, and of course on the other side gratitude for benefit conferred, I think that the basis of egalitarianism is simply the idea that all human beings share roughly the same sort of capacities and desires (over and above those that they have in common with other animals). Needless to say, there are striking differences between the capacities of an Einstein, or even a Lord Beeching, and those of the unskilled labourer who could barely learn to read and write at primary school. The striking differences are in capacities for action. The range of difference is much narrower, however, if you look at needs and the capacity for enjoyment. When it is a matter of distributing functions and responsibilities, obviously the relevant thing is what people are capable of doing. But these capacities are not *directly* relevant to the distribution of benefits. The money a man receives is used to satisfy his needs and his capacity for enjoyment. *Indirectly* the capacity for action is relevant because of the question of incentives for exercising capacities that are socially useful. The egalitarian is not blind to the range of differences in men's capacities for action. He is thinking of the lesser range of differences in their needs and capacity for enjoyment, and he believes that the monetary benefits which are used to meet needs and to give enjoyment should reflect that narrower range, not the less relevant wider range of differences in capacities for action. The utility and relative scarcity of managerial talent may justify incentives to a man to become a tycoon (does he really need a large monetary incentive if he has the qualities of character as well as intellect that make a good tycoon?), but it is not necessary and it is certainly not just that the Chairman of Shell should be paid £76,000 a year when many agricultural workers get less than £1,000. Everyone must agree with this in principle. Otherwise we would not have a tax system which reduces the tycoon's net pay to quite a small fraction of his gross pay, even when the gross figure comes nowhere near £76,000.

Granted then that it is morally offensive for a society to contain a wide span between the extremes of wealth and relative poverty, what can and should be done about it? When I lived in New Zealand just after the Second World War, there was a statutory minimum wage of £10 per week (with a purchasing power of perhaps £30 sterling at today's prices in Britain); and I was told that salaries in the public sector rarely exceeded twice that amount. If you were in business on your own account, you could of course earn a lot more. A society which has a free market economy cannot set an upper limit on the gross income that a man can earn. But it can fix a statutory minimum wage, and it can limit net incomes by its taxation policy. It can also control earnings, including the highest salaries, in the public sector, thereby setting an example of giving weight to the egalitarian principle of social justice along with the sometimes conflicting principle of social utility.

So far as taxation is concerned, the argument on the other side about disincentive effect is an argument against *high* rates of tax, not against an egalitarian policy as such. The argument is that a man will not do extra work, or will not save, if he gets only a small additional net return. But if he is allowed to retain a sizeable fraction of the money that his extra work or his investment has earned, he will not mind seeing the part that is taken away being used to bring poorer people a little nearer to his level. The very high rates of tax that are applied to some surtax-payers arise only because their incomes are ridiculously high. Conversely, ridiculously high additions to the salaries of top men, whether in the private or in the public sector, are due to the high rates of tax. If two thirds of a man's increment are going to be taken away in tax, his employers have to give him three times the amount they think he should have. So there is a vicious circle.

What is needed ideally is a linking of taxation policy with a wages and salaries policy. I do not know whether anything can be done in the private sector. But it strikes me as pretty silly that top Civil Servants now earn so much more than the political heads of their departments (and I do not mean that the pay of ministers should go up correspondingly). Talented young people who enter the Civil Service have always known that they could earn more in commerce or industry. They expect to have a good deal of material comfort, but if that were their sole or chief aim they would not choose the Civil Service. The salaries of Permanent Secretaries have gone up sharply in order that they should not be too far below those of the Chairmen of Boards for the nationalized industries, and the salaries of these gentlemen have gone up more sharply still so as not to lag behind private industry. In this respect we have been badly served by the public corporations. If the government thinks that wage increases in the public services should set an example to private industry, why not top salaries too?

However, it remains true that government in a free market economy cannot control salaries and wages in the way that it can control taxation. And if the objectionable thing is high rates of tax rather than redistribution of wealth, one needs to look out for alternative methods of reaching the aim. There could be more emphasis on expenditure taxes or on wealth taxes and less on income tax. Taxes on wealth need not be a disincentive to save if they do not run to high rates and if they concentrate on inherited wealth. After all it could be argued that inherited wealth is more of a disincentive to work than is income tax. These are matters for the economist, not the political philosopher. What emerges from my discussion of social justice is that the ethical position of socialists and radicals commands wider acceptance and is less bizarre in its theoretical grounding than appears at first sight.

4
Incentives, Distortion, and the System of Taxation

MAURICE PESTON*

Although the distinction between direct and indirect taxation continues to exist for administrative purposes, the economist has long since argued that it is of little value, and may, indeed, be rather misleading. Even the distinction between taxes on income and taxes on expenditure may not be particularly helpful, especially when it is realized that one tax on income, namely a tax on profits, may be shifted forward in higher prices by firms and, therefore, turns out to have much the same kind of effect as an explicit tax on expenditure. It is more sensible, therefore, to consider the effects of specific taxes and the bases on which they are levied rather than devote much time to the classification of taxes. What is more, since the relevant economic effects of a particular tax may be determined by what other taxes are levied, in many cases the correct approach will be in terms of the economic effects of a tax system. Actually, partly because the alternative to any tax change may be a change in the opposite direction of a transfer payment and partly because much other public expenditure has an effect akin to that of taxation, the ultimate objective should surely be an approach in terms of the overall system of taxation and expenditure in the public sector.

In this article I must limit myself to a much simpler objective, namely the discussion of certain incentive and distortion effects of taxation. All that I say, however, must be seen in this larger context. In particular, apart from what are conventionally recognized as taxes, it must be accepted that such things as national insurance and health contributions, the financial surpluses of nationalized industries, and user charges for public sector activi-

* The author is Professor of Economics at Queen Mary College in the University of London.

ties are all akin to taxes. (For that matter, the monopoly profit-element in some private-sector prices are akin to taxes, but not levied by the government.) In addition, although I leave the discussion of the distribution of income and capital to others, it must not be thought that I do not see this as the heart of the tax-reform problem.

Having said that, one enters into this field with considerable trepidation. One reason is that it is extremely complex. The economist sees many more problems than he can solve and elaborates much more theory than he can apply. Apart from that, the topics to be studied are full of controversy.

The Effect of Taxation on Incentives

At the centre of all this controversy lies the problem of taxation and the supply of effort. Now there can be no subject on which the plain man has more definite or more confident opinions than the disincentive effects of income tax. It is quite extraordinary how widely held this belief in disincentives is. Indeed, the more cynical ones amongst us, on the general theory that strength of everyday belief varies inversely with evidence, would infer from this alone that there is no foundation, in fact, for the disincentive effect.

It is nonetheless worthwhile examining much more closely the nature of the problem, the theory that has been applied to it, and the empirical results that research has realized.

Let us start with the supply of effort. In elementary economics this is taken to mean the number of hours worked. An analysis more relevant to the real world, however, would have to note that effort is multi-dimensional and includes some or all of the following: (*a*) number of hours worked; (*b*) intensity of work in those hours; (*c*) quality of work in those hours; (*d*) choice of occupation; (*e*) choice of geographical location; (*f*) attitude to promotion and responsibility; (*g*) attitude to additional education and training; (*h*) propensity to enter the labour force; (*i*) propensity to leave the labour force.

In addition. there are two kinds of dynamic issue to be taken into account. The supply of effort under any one of these headings may be affected more or less rapidly by a change in taxation, and the extent and nature of the response may vary with the life history or age of the person concerned. Thus, variations in hours worked or the pace of work may require a union agreement, and any effect on willingness to accept promotion will not be the same for a young man as for an older one.

More generally, if we partition the labour force in terms of sex, age, skills, training and education, location, industry, etc., it is possible, if not likely, that they will differ in their response to changes in the tax system, and for each of them that response will be made up of many different parts.

This takes us on to the next problem which concerns income or, more generally, the returns from work. To refer again to elementary economics, the decision problem examined there is the work-leisure choice, the latter being pleasurable, the former being unpleasant and needing to be compensated for by income. It is in a way rather curious that the central problem should be formulated in these terms by university teachers of economics, much of whose work must be (in my case, certainly is) extremely pleasurable. Nowadays, one would surely argue that a great deal of work, or being at work, is pleasurable and being at home is not. The traditional view of home being where you play and the factory where you work, might, in the light of restrictive practices on the one hand, and child-minding, washing-up, and repair work on the other, be precisely reversed. What is apparent is that the return from working is not simply income as narrowly defined, but includes items in kind (from luncheon vouchers to trips abroad), power, prestige, security, and an almost endless list of interests and pleasures.

Income itself must, of course, be interpreted in the broadest possible terms to include all the monetary returns to work over the lifetime of the worker. It includes all capital gains, all pension rights, and any other special concessions of a monetary kind connected with the job. (In technical economic terms we are concerned with the discounted present value of the additions to human wealth resulting from work.)

Taxes in Relation to Benefits

Thirdly, there is the characterization of the tax system. Even this turns out not to be as simple a matter as might be imagined. There are, first of all, the well-known complexities of the system of income and capital-gains taxation connected with the definitions of income and capital gains, and of what are regarded as costs allowed before arriving at taxable income. Especially important in this context are lump sums payable on retirement and subsequent pensions. This means that income-tax tables which show average tax rates of 80 per cent and marginal tax rates of 90 per cent for people earning £50,000 a year are most misleading. Economic analysis is not needed to reach this conclusion. All one has to do is to ask how, despite these so-called penal tax-rates, vast fortunes continue to be amassed, and expensive properties and motorcars continue to be purchased. Less well known but brought into prominence by recent discussion is the point that reductions of benefits are the same as increases in tax, and, therefore, that reductions in benefits that follow from income increases are the same as income taxes. All sorts of benefits come into this category varying from rent subsidies to council tenants to grants for students. The low-income deficiency scheme introduced by the government at the beginning of 1971 is precisely of this kind. A fascinating point is that the marginal tax rates (i.e., benefit reductions) of these schemes are frequently at the rate of 50 per cent and more, the level erroneously thought only to apply to people earning at least £6,000 a year.

The Influence of Age and Duration

Apart from that, there is yet another dynamic point worth making, and that concerns whether any particular tax change is thought to be temporary or permanent. The lifetime effect of a temporary tax change will obviously be smaller than a permanent one, and will have less powerful consequences (whatever they may be). Moreover, a tax change of any given duration will be

61

more significant to someone whose remaining working life is shorter than to a younger man who has a longer working life ahead of him. At the same time, the latter may have more options for change available to him than the former.

Finally, it must be emphasized again that incentive effects are not restricted to income taxes but may arise from so-called indirect taxes too. The taxation of commodities particularly wanted for leisure purposes may lower the value of leisure and cause people to be willing to work longer hours or more intensively. Paradoxically, they may do so in order to afford these leisure goods. Alternatively, they may choose a less commodity-intensive form of leisure, and simply earn less to enjoy more leisure hours as such.

To summarize, the three crucial elements in the discussion of incentives, namely, the supply of effort, the nature of income, and the tax system itself all turn out to be immensely complex. For this, if for no other reason, one must be most suspicious of anybody who claims to know that the tax system has certain quite definite overall incentive or disincentive effects. It is surely much more likely that a particular tax change will have an incentive effect for some and a disincentive for others, the nature of the effect also varying between individuals.

Diverse Responses

To revert to the effect of age on the nature of the response, a young person without family responsibilities may find a particular tax rate a disincentive to effort, a young family man may find the same tax rate an incentive, and an older person might again be in the disincentive category (unless, of course, his retirement pension depended on his gross salary). Similarly, a person whose gross income scale does not depend on his present efforts, i.e. one for whom promotion is not a normal phenomenon, will only lose current income if he works less or less well as a result of a tax change. But where promotion is significant the costs of less effort are much larger. Thus, a young ambitious man with promotion prospects will not find a tax increase a disincentive, while an older man who has already had all his promotion may well do so. (Incidentally, if the disincentive effects of high marginal tax rates were to be found in earlier retirements, would it be universally agreed that this was a bad thing?)

The number of different examples is enormous, and it would take a whole volume to mention them all. My purpose here, however, is simply to establish the point that they exist, and that many of them involve more subtleties than at first meet the eye. I cannot resist, nonetheless, consideration of one further example, university teachers. The *simpliste* disincentive argument would be that high marginal rates will cause them to work less and enjoy more leisure, while in the long run being less willing to accept promotion. (If the number of posts at all levels remains the same this will have no effect on the extent of promotion, but it may affect who gets or accepts promotion.) This, however, ignores the fact that a university teacher engages in a variety of activities so that the disincentive effect can occur in different ways. It may cause him to engage in less outside-consulting and spend more time on internal teaching and research. If there is a disincentive effect related to promotion, and this in turn is a function of research, he may research less and teach more. Alternatively, if income and promotion matter more to him, he may research more and engage in more outside activities of a paid kind while dropping those of an unpaid kind. Only as a result of a social cost-benefit analysis of all these consequences can we really determine and evaluate all the possible changes in work effort.

The Empirical Evidence

It is not surprising in an area as complicated as this that the empirical evidence is unclear and comparatively scarce. It is surprising, considering all the fuss that is made about the subject, that so little hard evidence on disincentives has been discovered. While it may be agreed that most of the studies which have so far been carried out in the UK and US are somewhat lacking in sophistication, and that there is an urgent need for more subtle empirical investigations in this field, there can be no doubt that they would have revealed what may be called gross disincentives if these exist on a large scale. In fact, they tend to turn up more examples of the tax system acting as an incentive to effort rather than as a disincentive. Moreover, the investigators cannot be accused of bias because some of them had quite clearly set out to discover cases of disincentives if these could be found.

What the investigations show is that people *think* the tax system is a disincentive in the sense that they believe it acts adversely on the work effort of others but not themselves. A survey in a national newspaper last year revealed this clearly, if unintentionally, by asking people whether they thought taxes were a disincentive and, not surprisingly, a majority answered in the affirmative. Unfortunately, the sample were not asked the relevant questions, namely, whether the tax system acted as a disincentive *to them and in what ways*. Related to this is what may be called – 'the Break effect' – after the economist who discovered it. If the theory of the effects of taxation is explained to people, and it is shown that if you value income highly it is sensible for you to work harder after tax rates are increased, many more of them, seeing the point, then agree that there are no disincentive effects to higher tax rates. In other words, in an initial interview they repeat the vulgar economics of the Press and television, because they cannot think of a rationale for a different view. Once given that rationale they are willing to look again at their own experience and reinterpret it.

My own casual observation confirms this. For many years I have given occasional lectures on the economy to Civil Servants and middle and senior managements. They always raise the question of the disincentive effects of taxation and are unanimous that they exist. But I have not found a single case of a person who will admit that such disincentives work for him. Indeed, such suggestions are regarded as preposterous, not to say insulting. In addition, I regularly plead for documented examples of disincentives to others, and these too are most noteworthy for their absence. In the end, all one is offered is hearsay.

A last point on disincentives is to note that they are alleged to exist all over the world, despite the great variations in income-

tax rates in different countries. A great deal of fuss is made on this matter in the US, for example, and yet the effective rate of tax on incomes, including capital gains, up to a million dollars a year hardly exceeds 30 per cent. There have also been a number of studies, chiefly emanating from the US, on the effects of direct taxes on economic growth. These derive from the early 1960s when US growth appeared to be lagging behind other areas, notably the Common Market, and it was thought that this might be attributable to a greater reliance on indirect taxes in faster-growing countries. It turned out that no systematic connection could be established between the direct-indirect tax mix, if that can be defined satisfactorily, and economic growth. One is tempted to believe, therefore, that we are more involved with special pleading and a not unexpected desire on the part of the better-off to hold on to their incomes, rather than with serious evidence on genuine economic effects. As far as Chancellors of the Exchequer are concerned, both Mr Barber and Mr Jenkins seem to have fallen for a myth rather than the harsh reality which is supposed to be the stock-in-trade of the Treasury.

Distortion Effects of Taxation

I turn now to the other part of the story, the distortions which the tax system is supposed to produce. This story, too, is by way of being a paradox. The economist has a remarkable tendency to view as distortions what the rest of us would regard as simple reality. The most absurd example of this is his treatment of the effects of spatial location as distortions, having defined his perfect economy as having no spatial dimensions at all. As far as the public sector is concerned, he discovers so-called public goods (defence and law and order being the most obvious, but there are many others) which must be provided by the state and be tax-financed. He then goes on to treat these taxes as distortions of the perfect working of the system. He even formulates the problem of the optimum tax structure in such a way that there are welfare losses attributable to such an optimum.

With that as background let us consider what distortions he

may mean, bearing in mind that these may be the inevitable consequences of available taxes which must be used to finance desirable public expenditure.

We can consider the distorting effect of the tax system by seeing how distortions arise in the economic system. They arise because decision-makers do not take the costs and benefits determined by their decisions correctly and fully into account. What appear to be costs to them may not be costs to the economy. What they see as benefits may not be a true reflection of the benefits to the economy. Moreover, there may be no other adjustments in the economic system to offset these imperfections. The standard examples of such distortions are monopoly profits and external economies and diseconomies. Monopoly profits enter into the costs of goods and services used in the economy, and are interpreted by their users as costs although they are not such to the economy as a whole. External economies are the free benefits given to others by good social behaviour of some people. External diseconomies are the costs imposed on others by bad social behaviour of some people. The construction of pleasant buildings is an example of the former; the pollution of the environment an example of the latter. If we make the usual economic assumption that decision-makers are selfish and only concern themselves with the internal effects of their actions, so to speak, they will operate activities that generate external economies at too low a level and activities that generate external diseconomies at too high a level. In other words, they will construct too few pleasant buildings and pollute the environment excessively.

Taxes on goods and services are alleged to distort the economic system because they enter into the price of things that households and firms buy and are, therefore, treated by them as costs, and yet there is no economic activity to which they directly correspond. In its simplest form welfare economics is about an economy in which prices measure benefits received and costs measure benefits foregone. An optimum situation is reached when price is equal to marginal cost. Once taxes are introduced, however, prices and costs become distorted measures of benefits and disbenefits and optimality is removed.

Now it is clear that this kind of economics is very close to being fallacious. As we have remarked already, having defined optimality in a notional situation where there is no government, it seems to arrive at a conclusion that a different situation in which a government (with the need to tax) is both inevitable and desirable is somehow sub-optimal. To take an extreme case: a country may wish to defend itself and may find that the only way to finance the defence budget is through some customs duties. Since the country moves to a preferable situation by this policy, to refer to the customs duties as a distortion seems to involve an unhappy terminology, to say the least.

Taxes may offset Distortions

Apart from that, there is also the point that once other distortions exist, taxes themselves may be introduced to offset them. The obvious example concerns the external diseconomies we have already mentioned. Firms polluting rivers do not take this into account when deciding on their industrial processes, but can be moved to do so if the use of such processes is subject to tax. In the case of monopolies, they may be induced to lower their prices by appropriate subsidies while, at the same time, their extra profits may be removed by a discriminatory profits tax. (I am not advocating this as a feasible or optimal anti-monopoly policy, but merely making the point that taxes may remove rather than create distortions.)

This last point is part of what is now called the theory of second best. It can happen that there are distortions generated by some taxes which can be mitigated by the introduction of further taxes. Indeed, it is this which leads us to the crucial issue concerning distortions, namely, given what taxes are available to the economy, and given our desire to raise tax revenue for various purposes, is the existing structure of taxes the best possible, or does it involve 'unnecessary distortions'? This seems to me to be a very important question, but, like so much of economics, does not lead to any clear positive answer of an empirical kind. Unfortunately, in the UK not a great deal of research work is being undertaken in this field so that I am extremely pessimistic about this situation improving in the near future. To get matters into perspective, however, research in the US suggests tentatively that the adverse economic effects of a sub-optimal tax system can be measured in terms of an order of magnitude less than 1 per cent of national income.

Some Negative Conclusions

There are apart from that a number of negative points to be made which are quite useful. First, it is not the case that taxes on goods involve distortions while taxes on income do not. The effect of the former is to cause market prices not to reflect correctly the choice between different goods in terms of cost; the effect of the latter is to distort the choice between income (and what it may be used for) and leisure. Secondly, it is not necessarily the case that the introduction of a new tax is beneficial in that it enables us to lower some other tax or reduces its rate of increase. The welfare significance of a new tax depends on all its demand- and cost-interrelationships with the other goods and services in existence in the economy. This can only be discovered by a detailed consideration of particular cases, and precious little of that has been done in the UK. In particular, as long as some goods (notably leisure) and some incomes are not to be taxed, it is not the case that an equi-proportionate tax on all the remainder is likely to be optimal.

A theorem that economists have played around with for the last forty years is that the ratio of tax to price ought to vary inversely with the elasticity of demand for the good in question (i.e., the rate at which demand falls off for given percentage increases in price). It has a certain persuasive appeal when it is realized that the more inelastic demand is, the less we have to raise price to bring in a specified revenue. Unfortunately, the strict conditions which have to be met for the theorem to hold are not those of our actual economy, and it has not so far been established how far the theorem has to be modified to allow for the difference between theory and reality.

Taxable Capacity

One reason for considering new taxes and the desirability of broadening the base of taxation is the so-called problem of the buoyancy of the revenue. It is sometimes suggested that additional sources of taxation must be brought into use, even if they lead to distortions of the economic system, simply because there may be no other way to raise the revenue to finance government expenditure and maintain the economy in equilibrium. All one can say about this is that while there may well exist something called taxable capacity either for the economy or for particular sectors of the economy, nobody has yet established what it is in the UK or what its likely effects are. We have mentioned already the lack of a direct connection between taxation and growth. We must mention now, despite the great interest in the hypothesis, the failure to establish a connection between taxable capacity (alleged to equal 25 per cent of national income) and inflation. This does not mean that the Treasury is mistaken in seeking new sources of public sector finance. It does mean that the distortion arguments must continue to be taken seriously.

Consider the current discussion of user charges for museums, art galleries, and libraries. If an additional user raises the costs of these institutions either because of his particular demands or because demand at zero price is so high that congestion results, it will be right to introduce a user charge unless its administrative cost swamps the resulting benefits. If, however, there is no congestion and no special costs attributable to extra individual users (i.e. the typical situation in these institutions most of the time), there will be a loss of welfare if charges are introduced. An additional viewer of a painting will gain because the painting is there, and he imposes no costs whatsoever on the system by looking at it. (Second-best arguments about charging elsewhere do not apply because of our assumption of zero costs.)

Of course, there are costs of new acquisitions and of using these institutions, but they are not attributable to their rate of use. The reason for introducing charges, therefore, may be that the taxes required to cover these costs involved greater distortions than do these user charges (i.e., that they do less damage at the margin than the present income tax), or that we have reached the limit of taxable capacity. (There may be another reason, namely, the desire to take some money from foreign visitors, which I shall not go into.) For this to hold, however, evidence of distortion and tax exhaustion must be introduced. In addition, the user charges must actually be employed to pay for additional acquisitions and meet the cost of running these places under existing or improved conditions.

To conclude, the tax field is controversial and full of people with axes to grind. It is a vital matter and yet does not receive the attention and research effort it deserves. There are serious problems of the effects of taxes on the way the economy works, and of the effects of these on economic welfare. Economic analysis and research help us to clarify some of these problems and to reject certain extreme positions. But in endeavouring to make policy and adopt a more constructive approach it is necessary to proceed with caution.

5
Poverty and Taxation

DAVID PIACHAUD*

During the past five years there has been much discussion of
alternative means of solving the poverty problem by giving poor
families extra money. Countless schemes for higher family allowances, negative income taxes, income guarantees and social dividends have been suggested, many as panaceas obscuring the real
issues. One remarkable feature of this discussion has been the
lack of attention given to the burden of taxes paid by the poor.
Indeed, the role of taxation as a direct cause of poverty has been
largely ignored. When a broader view is taken of the whole array
of taxes and income-related benefits, it becomes clear that there is
little scope for tackling poverty, redistributing incomes and reducing inequalities by means of any of the proposed schemes,
unless tax rates for the majority of the population are substantially increased. At present, and increasingly, the poor face
higher tax rates than any other section of the population and
many are effectively prevented by the system of taxation and
means-tested benefits from being able to raise themselves out of
poverty.

The Poverty Level

The poverty level we shall use is based on the Supplementary
Benefits Commission's rates, introduced in September 1971.
These rates indicate the minimum guaranteed by the government

*The author graduated in PPE at Oxford and took a Master's degree in
public administration in the University of Michigan at Ann Arbor. He
served as an economist in the Department of Health and Social Security
1968–70 and is now a lecturer in social administration at the London
School of Economics.

to those not at work – the retired, sick, unemployed and others – and can serve as a working definition of poverty. The incomes of those at work cannot be compared directly with these rates for two reasons. First, supplementary benefit rates are designed exclusively to meet the needs of those who are not in full-time work. Secondly, supplementary benefit payments are tax-free.

The process of going to work normally involves expenditure. First, there is the cost of travel to work, possibly also of special clothing and tools; this cost varies considerably from person to person, but let us assume a modest cost of 40 pence per week. Secondly, national insurance contributions have to be paid. Thirdly, there may be income tax to be paid. On the other hand, receipt of basic supplementary benefits and allowances acts as an entrée for other provisions. Most important of these is provision for rates and rent, or rates and interest on a mortgage (subject to a maximum for each area). We will assume a rent of £2.50 for households of every size and rates of 85 pence per week. (To meet commonly accepted space standards, larger families would in fact have to pay higher rents if they were to acquire the extra space needed.) Households dependent on supplementary benefits for long periods of time receive an addition to the basic rates of 50 pence per week. Moreover, while supplementary benefit recipients are entitled to free school meals, for others payment is based on a means-test, and such payments must be allowed for in comparing their incomes with the poverty level. On the basis of these assumptions the poverty levels for illustrative households are as shown in Table 1.

Table 1 Poverty Levels

	Net Income*
Single householders	£ 8.80
Married couple	£12.45
2–child family (children aged 8, 10)	£16.45
4–child family (children aged 6, 8, 10, 12)	£20.90

*Including provision for rent but after deducting payments for rates.

Taxing the Poor

Since Pitt's day, the first slice of income has been exempted from income tax. Since the free-trade era, food has been exempt from indirect taxation or treated particularly favourably. Among the reasons given for this special treatment of food has been the fact that food bulks largest in the expenditures of poor families. It is therefore popularly assumed that the tax system favours or even excludes the poor, or at least the poor who do not indulge in such 'vices' as smoking or drinking. But the facts are very different.

As will be shown, relative to incomes, the first slice exempted from income tax has been shrinking so that now income tax is payable even before households reach their poverty level. In addition to income tax, poor households are liable to local authority rates, but these are not the only elements of the tax system which we need to consider.

Housing is subject to a burden of local indirect taxation (rates). Insofar as families with children need to purchase more housing space, the burden of additional rates makes it that much harder for them to do so. For many this burden operates as a negative family allowance; for everyone it represents a steeply regressive tax; the lower the income, the higher the proportion taken in rates.

National insurance contributions are like taxes insofar as they are also compulsory levies, and like insurance only insofar as the right to specific benefits is purchased by the payment of these levies. Graduated national insurance contributions are payable on earnings above £9 per week – below the poverty level for all households – but the bulk of these contributions is made up of a flat-rate element which inevitably bears most heavily on the poorest households.

While family allowances are not usually regarded as part of the tax system, they have the same effect as child tax allowances in augmenting the spending power of families with two or more children. They are of course subject to tax. A fair assessment of net income requires us to take into account what the government provides as well as what is taken away by taxation.

The interrelation of tax and family allowances was demonstrated when the 1968 increases in family allowances were accompanied by 'clawback'. Child tax-allowances were reduced so that better-off families paid extra tax equal to the increase in their family allowances and therefore did not gain; poorer families benefited from the full increase in family allowances. Instead of increasing family allowances with 'clawback' in 1968, the government could have introduced a means-tested benefit for the same net cost which went only to low-income families. With appropriate scales, the same distributional effect could, in theory, have been achieved. In practice the operation of a means-tested benefit would, of course, differ substantially from the clawback method which uses the income tax system as a form of means-test to prevent benefits being extended up the income scale. (The apparent lower cost of a means-tested scheme is a delusion resulting from a quirk of government accounting.)

In August 1971 the government introduced a means-tested income supplement for families in preference to an extension of family allowances with clawback – the family income supplement. It remains to be seen how many of those eligible will in fact apply for the means-tested benefit, but it will be assumed here that families receive their entitlement. Means-tested benefits and cash payments like family allowances are rarely thought of as part of the tax system. But this separation is quite arbitrary. For example, rates are conventionally viewed as a tax, and rate rebates as a means-tested benefit: since the actual sum paid in rates is the difference between the full rates and any rebate, the two are inseparably linked; to put them into two different categories is artificial and unhelpful.

There are literally dozens of means-tested benefits and it has been estimated that over 1,500 different methods of means-testing are used by different local authorities and central government departments.[1] Most of these only come into operation when there is a special need, such as for a home help, or a school-uniform allowance, but many households, particularly those with children, may in normal circumstances be eligible for four or five

1. M. Reddin in '*Social Services for all?*', Fabian Society, 1968.

means-tested benefits. For simplicity only three means-tested benefits, for which virtually all households with children of school age are potentially eligible, will be discussed in conjunction with the tax system – family income supplement, rate rebates and school meals charges which, as pointed out above, must be taken into account in comparing the incomes of those at work with the poverty level.

Taking into account income tax, national insurance contributions, family allowances and these three means-tested benefits, we shall first consider how, at the end of 1971, the tax system affected households at or below the poverty level.

Table 2 Tax Thresholds

	Poverty level	Net income at tax threshold
Single person	£ 8.80	£ 6.33
Married couple	£12.45	£ 9.66
2–child family (children aged 8, 10)	£16.45	£16.54
4–child family (children aged 6, 8, 10, 12)	£20.90	£21.62

The comparison is made in Table 2 between the net income at the tax threshold and the poverty level for families of different size. In the case of a married couple, income tax starts to be paid when earnings reach £11.50 per week giving a net income (after national insurance, rebated rates and work expenses) of only £9.66 per week, £2.79 below the poverty level. Only personal tax allowances are allowed for in calculating tax thresholds in Table 2. But at these levels of income few households are likely to be entitled to other tax allowances such as life insurance or mortgage-interest relief. The budgets of 1969 and 1970 gave relief to the low-income tax-payer by raising personal tax allowances. The reduced-rate tax bands were reduced in 1969 and eliminated in 1970. The budget of 1971 raised child tax-allowances, thereby raising the tax threshold for most larger families above the poverty level. For the majority of households, however, income tax still starts to be paid before the poverty level is reached.

The Royal Commission on the Taxation of Profits and Income[2] laid down a clear principle for the tax threshold: 'There should be no income tax levied upon any income which is insufficient to provide its owner with what he requires for subsistence.' By subsistence was meant 'an income large enough to equip and sustain a healthy and efficient citizen'. Presumably the level of supplementary benefit scales is chosen with a similar objective. Indeed it would be hard to defend a higher minimum for the giving of tax-financed allowances through the Supplementary Benefits Commission than for tax threshold purposes. Nevertheless, the current tax threshold is for most households lower than the level of living provided by the Supplementary Benefits Commission.

At present, a married couple requires earnings of £16.40 per week to reach the poverty level (see Table 3); with these earnings they would be paying £1.48 in income tax, £1.22 in national insurance contributions, and £0.85 in rates, a total of £3.55 per week. A 4-child family with a rent of only £2.50 per week needs to earn over £20 per week to reach the poverty level; if their rent were £8 per week (a modest rent for such a family arriving in London) the earnings required to reach the poverty level would be £28, at which level these taxes would amount to over £4 per week.

The fact that many people end up substantially below the poverty level despite a full week's work is in large measure due to income tax, national insurance and rates. This is clearly indicated in Table 3 (opposite).

Marginal 'Tax' Rates

The impact of taxation on the poor can be considered from another angle. The majority of the working population pay income tax at the standard rate (30 per cent after allowing for

2. Second Report, Cmnd. 9105, HMSO, 1954, para. 158.

Table 3 Earnings Required to Reach Poverty Level

	Earnings required to reach poverty level	Family allowances	Family income supplement	Income tax	N.I.* contribution	Rates (after rebate)	Expenses of employment	Net income (equals poverty level)
Single person	£12.40	—	—	1.32	1.03	0.85	0.40	8.80
Married couple	£16.40	—	—	1.48	1.22	0.85	0.40	12.45
2-child family (children 8, 10)	£17.04	0.90	1.03	—	1.27	0.85	0.40	16.45
4-child family (children aged 6, 8, 10, 12)	£20.24	2.90	0.43	—	1.42	0.85	0.40	20.90

*Including industrial injuries and national health service contributions.

Table 4 Marginal 'Tax' Rates

2-Child Family (Children aged 8, 10)

Earnings	Family income supplement	Income tax	N.I.* contribution	Rates	School meal charges	NET** INCOME	Marginal 'tax' rate
£15	2.05	—	1.18	0.43	—	15.94	—
£16	1.55	—	1.22	0.59	—	16.24	70%
£17	1.05	—	1.27	0.85	—	16.43	81%
£18	0.55	0.23	1.32	0.85	—	16.65	78%
£19	—	0.53	1.37	0.85	—	16.75	90%
£20	—	0.84	1.42	0.85	—	17.39	36%
£21	—	1.14	1.46	0.85	0.60	17.45	94%
£22	—	1.44	1.51	0.85	1.20	17.50	95%
£23	—	1.74	1.55	0.85	1.20	18.16	34%

4-Child Family (Children aged 6, 8, 10, 12)

Earnings	Family income supplement	Income tax	N.I.* contribution	Rates	School meal charges	NET** INCOME	Marginal 'tax' rate
£17	2.05	—	1.27	0.43	—	19.85	—
£18	1.55	—	1.32	0.59	—	20.14	71%
£19	1.05	—	1.37	0.85	—	20.33	81%
£20	0.55	—	1.42	0.85	—	20.78	55%
£21	—	—	1.46	0.85	—	21.19	59%
£22	—	0.17	1.51	0.85	—	21.97	32%
£23	—	0.47	1.55	0.85	—	22.63	34%
£24	—	0.77	1.59	0.85	1.20	22.09	154%
£25	—	1.08	1.64	0.85	1.80	22.13	96%
£26	—	1.38	1.69	0.85	2.40	22.18	95%
£27	—	1.68	1.73	0.85	2.40	22.84	34%

*Including industrial injuries and national health service contributions.
**Including family allowance, less expenses of employment.

earned income relief) and pay graduated national insurance contributions. Together they now result in a marginal rate of deduction of about 35 per cent.

Families with children suffer a further loss of marginal income
because of the loss of family income supplement and free school
meals. The net incomes of 2- and 4-children families with
different levels of earnings are shown in Table 4. By comparing
the changes in net income with the changes in earnings the marginal loss of income or 'tax' can be calculated. (The marginal tax
rate is the proportion of any increase in income that goes in tax.)
A 2-child family earning £20 per week receives school meals free
of charge; when earnings reach £21 per week the meals for 1
child have to be paid for at a cost of 60 pence per week during
school term-time. Added to the effect of income tax and graduated national insurance contributions this creates a marginal 'tax'
rate of 94 per cent. If this family increases its earnings from £20
to £22 per week it will end up only 11 pence per week better off.
A family which increases its earnings by £7 per week, from £15
to £22 per week, will end up only £1.54 per week better off.

In the case of a 4-child family the situation is even worse. An
increase in earnings from £17 to £27 per week makes this family
£2.99 per week better off. Over this £10 range of earnings there
is an average marginal 'tax' rate of 70 per cent. An increase in
earnings from £23 to £26 per week would result in this family
actually being worse off by 45 pence per week.

The poorest households may be little or no better off by earning more: not only will they have to pay more tax but they will
also have to pay for benefits which they previously received free.
Despite all the talk about the importance of incentives to management, nothing as harsh as this happens to people with very
high earnings.

The 1971 budget reduced the highest marginal tax rate for those
with incomes over £20,000 per annum to 75 per cent: at the same
time it served to raise the tax rates on the poorest households.

Getting out of poverty is like getting out of a well. Unless you
can jump right to the top you will slip back to precisely where

you started. One wonders how many people are aware of this and give up the effort to earn more. What people cannot fail to realize is the number of different local and central government departments to whom information must be provided if all benefits are to be claimed. Indeed, the task of claiming and reclaiming is such that many households do not claim and fail to receive their entitlements. Failure to claim benefits reduces marginal 'tax' rates, but at the cost of increasing the extent and severity of poverty.

The road which has led to this situation has been paved with good intentions. Each new means-tested scheme was introduced if not to benefit the poorest households, at least to shelter them from some new charge, or from an increase in an established charge. But the burden of these charges, from which the poorest have been exempt, has dragged many more down to poverty. Each means-test appears to have been evolved by the particular central or local government department with scant regard to other means-tests. In this field coordinated action has been sadly lacking.

The current proliferation of charges for the social services, particularly for health services, with exemption for the low-paid, must inevitably result in increasing numbers of households being brought down to the poverty level.

It is against this sombre description of the present situation that the various 'solutions' to the poverty problem should be considered.

Proposed Solutions

Fostered perhaps by fascination at the idea of the Inland Revenue paying out money, of all the 'solutions' negative income tax has probably attracted the most adherents. As its name suggests, negative income tax is income tax in reverse. While a positive income tax takes money from those with incomes above the tax threshold a negative income tax would pay out money to those with incomes below it. The plan has fervent advocates. For example:

... the development and application of a system of negative taxation offers the brightest hope of emancipation from the doctrines of universality in social welfare that have militated so long against an implacable war on poverty.[3]

Despite the spell cast over some of its adherents, there is no special magic in using the income-tax machine to make up the income of those with low incomes. Precisely the same financial effect could be achieved by a flat-rate guaranteed income-payment or social dividend paid to all households, accompanied by a special tax, or by a means-tested benefit operated by a local or central government agency. The essential differences between these mechanisms are administrative and presentational, though the method of administration may be crucial in determining how many actually receive the money they are intended to get.

The theoretical advantages of a negative income tax are that it can make use of information already obtained, or believed to be already obtained, for a further socially useful purpose: that it would avoid the stigma of a separate means-tested benefit and avoid the 'give and take' of the present system, or the even greater giving and taking which would be involved in a guaranteed-income or social-divided scheme. For households whose work incomes are continuously covered by the Pay As You Earn system and have no other sources of income, the advantages of a negative income tax could, in theory at least, be realized without any great administrative problem. The really formidable difficulties arise with households outside the PAYE system, whether temporarily (e.g. the sick and unemployed, those changing jobs) or permanently (e.g. over two million self-employed), or below the PAYE threshold (e.g. part-time earnings of wives). Immense practical obstacles have to be overcome before such a system covering the entire population could provide negative tax payments each week or month related to current circumstances; it would seem to require the computerization of income tax and of all payments, however small, to all employees, which would

3. D. Lees, 'Poor Families and Fiscal Reform', *Lloyds Bank Review*, October 1967.

take many years to develop. But even this would not bring in the self-employed.

A system of guaranteed social dividend flat-rate payments could be introduced far more quickly and would almost certainly involve the lowest administrative cost. It is the resentment likely to be caused by 'taking' so much more in taxation, despite the 'giving' of greater benefits, which makes it politically unattractive. In the distant future the social advantages of a guaranteed income for all may, perhaps, come to be realized.

The Real Issues

The real issues of principle posed by negative income tax and means-tested schemes have unfortunately been obscured by ideological commitments to particular administrative techniques of achieving the redistribution of income, which so many people say they wish to see achieved. But this apparent agreement on objectives would probably prove to be illusory if answers were sought to the important question of which existing mechanism or mechanisms for redistribution the new system was intended to replace. It certainly cannot be simply superimposed on all the existing means-tested allowances, rebates and remissions, without leading to intolerable consequences. As shown above, many families already gain little from earning more. Yet another income-related benefit on top of all the others would make it pay to earn less. Moreover, the system would become even more complicated and hard for families to comprehend and operate than it is at present. Some part of the present system, therefore, must clearly be replaced.

A second important question to be answered is how a negative tax system can be made compatible with the principles of national insurance. The short answer is that it cannot. It is difficult enough to defend the provision of supplementary benefit alongside national insurance if the principle of payment in return for contribution is to be maintained. If everyone automatically received a negative income-tax payment, how could one maintain the principle that social insurance was 'earned' by contributions?

Third, what should the negative tax rate be? If the same allowances were used for both the payment of positive tax and the receipt of negative tax – as would be essential in practice – the positive and negative tax rates would determine the value of the allowances. Thus if the tax allowance for each child were £200 and the negative tax rate 50 per cent, for the lowest income levels receiving negative tax the 'benefit' for a child would be £100 per year; to those better off paying positive tax at, say, 30 per cent, the 'benefit' for a child would be only £60 per year. At present the 'benefit' for a child (the combined value of allowances, family income supplement and child tax-allowances) varies with income, being lowest for middle-income households. For most households the 'benefit' for each child is less than the supplementary benefit/poverty level allowance for each child. It is for this reason, as was shown earlier (Table 3), that the earnings required to reach the poverty level are so high in large families, and this is why, in practice, poverty has the highest incidence among these families.

Thus before any reconstruction of the system can be considered, the following fundamental questions must be answered. What should be the total 'benefit' for a child and how should this vary with income? In other words, what proportion of the 'cost' of a child should the state provide to poor families? Expenditure on children increases with income; should more be provided for children in better-off families or can such families be expected to meet a larger proportion of the cost themselves? Should the same provision be made by the government for each child in a family, whether the first or the sixth, and should this provision vary with the age of each child? In general, how far should incomes be based on raw market-forces and how far on needs? These questions are clearly not easy to answer; but they need to be faced rather than merely take over the answers implied in one or another of the schemes that have been put forward.

Redistributing Income

For the poor to benefit from a redistribution of income through the tax system, either the burden of taxation that now falls on them must be reduced or the benefits they receive must be increased – or both. To reduce the burden of taxation on the poor through a general reduction of taxation for all (as would result, for example, from a reduction in flat-rate national insurance contributions) would be an improvement but it would not result in any narrowing of the gap between the poor and other households. To give tax reductions only to the poor would require higher tax rates on those better off, assuming the same level of public expenditure. If higher means-tested benefits were given to the poor, and to the poor only, the extra means-test would result in higher marginal 'tax' rates for the poor and make it yet harder for the poorest to raise themselves out of poverty. This could only be avoided by giving the benefit also to those above the poverty line. The withdrawal of this benefit through a test of means would have to start considerably above the poverty line, to avoid overlapping with the range of income over which present benefits for the poor are being withdrawn. But this would enormously increase the cost of the scheme and the number of families who would have to be means-tested, as well as the marginal 'tax' rates of these families. Thus it would be administratively easier and not much more expensive to help the poor by providing more or higher benefits on a universal basis (e.g. increased family allowances) financed by higher rates of taxation on middle and upper income groups. Either way, the marginal tax rates of those on middle and high incomes would have to be increased substantially. It is no wonder that it has proved difficult for governments to find a politically acceptable solution to the problem of poverty.

Two possible approaches to tackling poverty which arise out of consideration of the taxation of the poor may be briefly mentioned.

Many government provisions at present benefit the more affluent members of society. For example, the tax subsidy to owner-occupiers is greater in total and more per house than the tax subsidy to council tenants. Higher income groups utilize certain elements of the health and education system far more effectively than those less well-off. Publicity, education, and the provision of services in a manner which is convenient, acceptable and suited to all income levels can all reduce under-utilization of services. For example, to establish equal educational opportunity for all may require positive discrimination and compensatory programmes to help children from disadvantaged home backgrounds and a general broadening of the social base of the educational system. A wider utilization of the social services together with the elimination of those provisions which exclusively benefit the more affluent would help to reduce inequalities.

Redistribution must take new forms. Greater benefits for the poor should be provided not only on the basis of each individual's income but also on the basis of the needs of whole communities or districts; this may mean improving schools in twilight areas, a programme for housing improvements or the provision of new jobs in a community. Of course many who are not poor or in need will benefit from such general provision for poor areas and of course there are serious problems in selecting areas for preferential treatment. The alternatives are to do nothing or to exacerbate a system which already prevents many households from being able to help themselves out of poverty.

Both these approaches would require increased public expenditure, but not such as to require a major increase in standard-rate income tax: to suppose that poverty can be tackled and income redistributed without raising tax rates to some degree is illusory.

In the present climate of public opinion, increases in tax rates are not seen to be electorally advantageous. For this reason and because of the need to avoid further increases in the marginal 'tax' rates of those close to the poverty level, which already prevent many households from raising themselves out of poverty, it would appear that the political limit to redistribution through benefits and taxes related to each household's income is close to being reached. The expectation that adjustment of the tax system could of itself ever achieve a substantial change in the distribution of economic power is, perhaps, naïve.

6

Reform of the British Income Tax System

G. CLAYTON and R. W. HOUGHTON*

Whatever changes are made in the British tax system, the personal income tax is likely to remain its centrepiece as in most developed countries. The reason for this is clear: given the somewhat elaborate administrative machine required to operate the tax equitably, income tax has the considerable advantage that it can be closely adjusted to prevailing conceptions of ability to pay and indeed income has come to be regarded as the best *single* measure of ability to pay. Although *expenditure* on the one hand and *wealth* on the other provide alternative bases for a personal tax, neither is likely to usurp income, chiefly because of the disturbance involved in changing from the present to another tax base and of the need to establish a complex administrative machinery for assessment, which in the case of both the tax bases mentioned could not easily be made sufficiently comprehensive. It is a common misconception that the choice of the tax base inevitably leads to a precise definition of the tax. In fact the range of potential taxes on income is very large, being the product of the number of tax formulae (progressive, proportional, regressive, etc.) which can be applied and the number of definitions of income (tax bases) to which application of the formulae may be made. 'Income tax', a learned judge remarked, 'is a tax on income.' 'And by income', another explained, 'is meant such income as is within the Act taxable under the Act.'

The present United Kingdom tax system, in common with many other British institutions, has like Topsy 'just growed' and is the result of gradual evolution over a period of nearly two

*Professor Clayton is Chairman of the Division of Economic Studies in the University of Sheffield. Mr Houghton is a senior lecturer in economics in Sheffield University and editor of *Penguin Readings in Public Finance*.

hundred years. It has never been fundamentally revised but has been patched up and modified whenever demands for change have become so insistent that the natural conservatism and aversion to change of those charged with its administration has been overcome. It would be surprising if the failure to re-appraise the whole income tax system in the light of the transformation of the social and economic environment during such a long period had not given rise to major weaknesses and faults. The most recent major innovation in the British system was the taxation of capital gains, which had, by and large, previously been defined by judicial decision as not 'taxable under the Act'. Other important changes in recent times were the introduction of the 'clawback' principle to ensure that full standard-rate tax-payers received no net benefit from increased cash family allowances; the proposals in the 1968 budget for aggregating the investment income of minor children with that of their parents; and the introduction in the 1971 budget of an optional arrangement for the separate taxation of the earnings of married couples. Prior to this latter proposal the effect of combining their earnings had meant substantially higher surtax payments than if each were taken separately or than if each was assessed on one half of their joint earnings.

The reflection in its tax arrangements of a nation's social institution and the values placed on them by law-makers is a fascinating subject which it is not the object of this paper to pursue. We refer to this influence on tax arrangements only to underline the point that, insofar as social institutions and the relative values placed on them are subject to change through time, it is to be expected that any set of tax arrangements will eventually become at least partially obsolescent. Apart, therefore, from considerations of day-to-day administrative convenience, there is a presumption in favour of flexible institutions. Insofar as complexity is the enemy of flexibility it is to be discouraged and avoided wherever possible. It might well be argued that a personal income tax must of necessity be complex if a serious attempt is made to make it equitable. But in our view it would be nearer the truth to say that a complex system is inevitably inequitable and almost certainly inefficient and costly to administer. In what follows, a programme for the reform of the UK personal income-tax system is outlined which we believe is likely to produce important economic and social benefits. This is not an alternative to some proposals in the 1971 budget which have been hailed by many commentators as far-reaching but is a plan for the radical reform of the *whole* system, in which the essence of these proposals could be accommodated without much difficulty.

It is a fact of simple arithmetic that to raise a given amount of revenue requires a lower average *rate* of tax the larger is the tax base. The more comprehensive is the definition of income subject to tax, the lower can tax rates be. The price of narrowing the base, by defining certain kinds of receipts as not income for tax purposes or by granting allowances and reliefs, is an increase in tax rates. We have already noted that capital-gains taxation was a recent innovation in the UK. But gifts, inheritances and gambling winnings are not taxed. There is an important group of reliefs including personal allowances, allowances for wives, allowances for dependent children and business expenses which all serve to reduce taxable income. Taken together, these exemptions and deductions are sufficiently comprehensive to have a considerable impact. There are two important consequences. The first is that higher tax rates may have undesirable economic consequences, particularly in reducing the incentive to save and take risks, although it must be admitted that the widely held belief that the British income-tax system discourages effort owes more to emotion than to a cool appraisal of such empirical evidence (admittedly scanty) as we have. The second is that exclusions from tax may make the system less equitable.

The income tax is an annual tax, income being assessed and taxed yearly. This has important consequences for a progressive tax. Over an individual's lifetime, if tax rates are unchanged, the tax he will actually have to pay on a given total of income receipts will depend on its distribution through time and will be lower the more equally the total is dispersed over his tax-paying life. The steeper the degree of progression, the greater the penalty for having income 'bunched' in time. Such a tax has an inevitable bias against occupations with fluctuating earnings, such as authors have, and occupations which carry a high income for a relatively short number of years, such as those of professional footballers or athletes. There are two ways out of this obvious source of inequity: one is to have a proportional tax system, so that 'bunching' does not affect tax liability, the other is to drop the annual basis of assessment and to allow averaging, so that although the system is progressive with respect to a lifetime's income, it is not necessarily progressive with annual income. It used to be argued that capital gains could not be included in the UK tax base because realizations of assets are often 'bunched' in time (the fact of the 'bunching' of lifetime earnings of footballers and pop stars being conveniently ignored). Bunching is likely to be an even more striking characteristic of such windfalls as inheritances, winnings from gambling, and gifts. It is obvious that to apply the progressive rates of an annual tax to receipts which typically accrue so irregularly in time would be inequitable. But it is also inequitable to ignore them altogether, for many such gains (gambling winnings may be the exception) accrue mainly to the rich; the majority of them can only accrue to property owners, and amongst property owners the wealthiest hold a larger proportion of their assets in forms which benefit from gains. The answer adopted by the UK government was to use a special proportional tax on long-term gains and a similar solution could be adopted for inheritances, gambling winnings, and gifts. Mr James Callaghan, when Chancellor of the Exchequer, defended the exemption of gambling winnings on the logical grounds that as there was no capital asset there could be no capital gains. But no amount of semantics can disguise the fact that such an exemption conflicts with the objective of taxing spending-power which previously has avoided income tax. However, the wider the net is spread to catch various receipts, the less acceptable is the case for exempting them from the effects of the progressive income tax. For the sacrifice of progression means abandoning the more generally accepted criterion of ability to pay and makes the capital-gains tax a weak instrument for diminishing inequalities of wealth. A better answer would seem to be to include such receipts as income but to modify the annual basis and allow averaging over, say, five-year periods at least. Given such a wide and comprehensive interpretation of income, the tax base is not eroded and increases in required tax rates are avoided, as are the inequities inherent in a strictly annual basis of assessment. The inclusion of these receipts would eliminate the need for separate taxes on estates or inheritances, on gifts and on capital gains and, given the inclusion of receipts from these sources in taxable income, the need for a tax on wealth would, of course, be diminished.

Let us now turn to a consideration of the effects on the tax base of allowances. The exemption of a first small block of income from tax is a normal instrument of progression and thus of vertical equity. Whether justifiable or not, the earned income allowance is used in the UK system as a means of discriminating against investment income. Such discrimination can be defended on the grounds that the possession of capital, as well as the income which flows from it, shows additional taxable capacity, and in the absence of a proper wealth tax this differential is justified as a limited form of tax on capital. But if our proposals made above were accepted, the need to discriminate between earned and unearned income would be removed. This would have the advantage that much of the existing confusion about actual tax rates would be removed, for the majority of tax-payers act on the mistaken assumption that additional earned income will attract tax at the full standard rate. Even if our more radical proposals for reform failed to gain acceptance, it would be preferable to abolish the existing earned income relief and impose a surcharge on unearned income in its place.

With regard to the other major allowances in the UK tax system, namely those for a wife and dependent children, justification must be sought in considerations of horizontal equity. The extra allowance for a married man is a *curiosum* from an economic standpoint. Budget studies, as the Carter Commission on the Canadian tax system stressed, indicate that a man and woman 'sharing bed and board' live more cheaply than they would as single individuals although the more extreme argument, often employed by engaged couples, that 'two can live as cheaply as one', is not borne out. Thus, on grounds of ability to pay, marriage increases rather than reduces their joint taxable capacity so that a negative in place of a positive addition to his personal allowance is called for when a man marries. Apparently, the present arrangements in Britain reflect a Victorian bourgeois picture of a helpless and non-productive female passing from the state of being an economic liability of her father to that of being an economic liability of her husband. It might be objected that to turn the present tax advantage of marriage into a disadvantage would further discourage from marriage men and women who wish to live together and that this is undesirable on social and moral grounds, despite the fact that other provisions of the tax system have precisely this effect of providing financial incentives to 'live in sin'. Without pursuing this question further, it can be maintained that the cost to the revenue of the married man's additional personal allowance – some £500 million or the yield of a 5-per-cent income tax – is too high a price to be paid in homage to what is both a fast disappearing attitude and a minority situation. In this day and age the economic and social case for regarding marriage as such as a state of which the tax system should take cognizance seems weak.

The case of dependent children is different for many reasons. Human beings are economic agents and their productive efficiency depends on what has been invested in them to develop and train their innate skills and abilities; more than this, their contribution to the social well-being of their fellow citizens depends upon their social training and development. When the responsibility for ensuring that the abilities of children are developed to the full rests with parents (the argument loses much of its validity where social arrangements, such as those obtaining in a kibbutz, are different), there is an overwhelming case for the state to create conditions in which as far as possible the lack of parental income is not an obstacle to the achievement of social objectives. Thus, although there is no reason in the case of a childless married couple to make it financially easier through the tax system for the wife to remain at home (which is the effect of the married man's additional allowance), once there is a child or children, the extent to which the mother is tempted to supplement the family income by cutting down on time spent in caring for them should be minimized. This would suggest a policy of making available high family allowances for a first child for a minimum number of years, with perhaps rather lower allowances for subsequent children, although inequities would arise unless adjustments were made to cater for the different circumstances of families whose children are closely spaced in age and those whose children are not. Rates could be pitched at such a level that those women whose opportunity earnings were not high enough to employ adequate domestic help to look after their children would not have a considerable financial inducement to go out to work. At the same time the abolition of the married man's additional allowance would provide an income incentive for other women to enter or re-enter employment, and thus help maintain the active labour force by increasing participation rates. The importance to the British economy of ensuring that its human resources are efficiently developed and deployed is so obvious that it needs no elaboration.

A third conclusion of simple arithmetic is that so long as there are human resources whose productive capacities could be improved by giving them higher incomes and, at the same time, there are people whose disposable incomes could be reduced without reducing the social value of their outputs, then total national income can be increased by investment in human capital financed by means of the redistribution of income. This argument, however, may reasonably be said to prove too much. So long as the marginal productivity of investment of any kind of capital, human or non-human, is positive, it apparently justifies investment at the expense of consumption. It is unlikely that the general good requires investment to be carried as far as this: presumably there is an optimal cut-off point for investment in each category of capital, given by a non-zero rate of return. What has to be recognized at this point is that the imperfections of the capital market are such that there is a natural built-in bias against investment in human capital for, in general, funds for investment in the education and training of people may be less easily available than funds for other purposes. Evidence for this may be found in the so far insuperable difficulties encountered in devising schemes for the provision of loans for students financed by the private sector. One of the major obstacles is that investment in human beings does not provide collateral of a kind acceptable to financial institutions except in a society in which slavery is an acceptable institution. This brings us naturally to an examination of the case for the provision of loans to individuals by the state; we need to clear the ground for a thoroughgoing discussion of this.

We have already given convincing reasons why the uneven accrual of taxable income between time-periods can create undesirable inequities under a progressive tax system. What perhaps is less obvious but just as inequitable is that the unequal accretion of necessary expenditures can have exactly the same effect, unless the tax-payer is freely able to borrow and lend so that what is at his disposal corresponds to his necessary expenditure. An example is the use made by the higher income groups of insurance policies taken out on children at an early age to provide for their later education at boarding schools. Let us elaborate the point further. Under an income-tax system, taxable capacity is essentially the same as *discretionary income*, that is, actual income less necessary expenditure on self and dependents. This is recognized by the existing system of granting allowances. The deduction of these allowances from actual income determines taxable income, the application of the tax schedules determines tax liability *and also, under present arrangements, the amount of tax that is to be paid in the current year*. Now it may be that the tax-payer, using his foresight and contemplating the scale of his future commitments, would prefer to pay a lower amount of tax this year and more in subsequent years. This is a plausible situation for a man whose children have not completed their education and who feels that the whole family would benefit from, say, a leisurely and expensive foreign holiday, or living in a larger house. If he undertakes extra work in order to increase his

94

income to try to pay for such additional expenses, he will at the same time increase his current tax liability and current tax payments. The additional work and effort needed to produce the required net increase in disposable income may be just too much. In such circumstances the possibility of deferring the additional tax for, say, five years, at the cost of paying an agreed rate of interest to the government for the privilege, could produce a considerable improvement in welfare. Thus, not only is there a case for income-spreading on equity grounds, there is also a case for separating current tax liabilities and tax payments on the same grounds and perhaps to increase efficiency. Because the ownership of capital is so unequal, with the inevitable consequence that the opportunities for, and costs of, borrowing vary widely as between one individual and another, there is a case for tax loans to enable people to pay their taxes when they feel such payments will involve the least sacrifice of welfare. Moreover, insofar as loan facilities of this kind are used to improve the care and training of children or the productive capacities of adults, they may well produce social as well as private benefits.

Such a scheme for tax loans, while justifiable on welfare grounds, raises certain problems. In the first place, there is the danger of encouraging a 'Micawberish' attitude on the part of tax-payers so that they take a completely unrealistic view of their future abilities to meet their future tax liabilities and the repayment of tax loans. Secondly, if the right to defer tax payments were subject to no restrictions, it would be extremely difficult for the authorities to predict the tax yield for a given financial year and would render the problem of demand management that much more intractable. For these reasons it would appear desirable to limit the individual tax-payer's right to avail himself of the opportunity to postpone tax payments to an upper limit of his current tax liabilities. For example, it could be stipulated that an individual tax-payer would not be able to postpone more than 25 per cent of his current liability to tax by this device. Such an arbitrary rule would reduce the advantages on welfare grounds but would do something to reduce the force of the above arguments.

Another objection is that individual tax-payers would fail to make realistic allowances for the possibility of a catastrophic drop in earning power due to unemployment arising from such causes as redundancy. Since, given realistic full employment policies, such potential reasons for default would affect only a minority of tax-payers, it should be possible to incorporate in a scheme of tax loans an insurance surcharge to cover a possible loss of revenue arising from such eventualities.

However, the most serious objection of all arises from expectations of the future rate of inflation. Many sophisticated tax-payers, irrespective of their views about the optimum allocation of income over a period of years, would leap at the opportunity of paying current tax liabilities in a few years' time in a depreciated currency. This raises the very large question of the extent to which a government and its agencies should explicitly recognize the risk of inflation in formulating its policies. In this instance the case for so doing is compelling. One of the objections to the existing capital-gains tax is that, since the tax is on monetary and not on real gains, a man may pay tax although in real terms he has made a loss. There are strong arguments in favour of arranging that the rate of capital-gains tax should taper downwards over time in line with an acceptable price-index, as has been suggested by Professor A. R. Prest.[1] Such a reform could be combined with a scheme whereby tax loans would be repayable after adjustments to the original sum borrowed, to allow for inflation. During the post-war years, in which the majority of countries have experienced inflation in varying degrees, there has persisted a widespread belief that any scheme for value-linking in borrowing obligations is open to serious objections. First, there is the view that by implying a willingness to live with inflationary expectations rather than fighting them head-on, the use of such a device merely aggravates the position. It must be admitted that this is possible. Consequently, any decision by a government to use value-linking should be complemented by other fiscal and monetary policies which impress upon the public

1. A. R. Prest, *Public Finance in Theory and Practice*, Weidenfeld and Nicholson, 1967, Chap. 13.

that the decision is part and parcel of a disciplined economic policy and not one which can be interpreted as a sign of weakness. The second issue on which opinions differ is the effect which the acceptance of value-linking by the government would have on the capital market as a whole. There is a fear that the introduction of value-linking by the government, although on a small scale to begin with, would inevitably spread to all public borrowing and into private loan transactions as well. This fear seems frequently to be based on the assumption that a value-linked bond would carry the same nominal rate of interest as one which is not linked in this way. This should not be necessary. As the experiences of Israel and Finland show, it is practicable for value-linked and non-linked obligations to exist side by side provided that the respective interest-differential reflects price expectations. Since a full discussion of this issue would take us well beyond the subject of income tax reform, suffice it to say that a limited application of value-linking to transactions between the government and tax-payers would not necessarily have disastrous consequences for the capital market as a whole.

To further widen the British personal income-tax base the distinction between personal and company income could be dropped, and company profits, whether distributed or retained, taxed as the income of individual shareholders. The charge that the present distinction merely recognizes the well-known schism between ownership and control merely invites the retort that it helps to perpetuate it. If retained profits were taxed simply as shareholders' income, shareholders would have a much greater incentive to ensure that they were well-used. A general point is illustrated when, as in this case, there is a different tax treatment of items that are to any extent interchangeable; the inevitable result is that resources are devoted to maximizing those that are taxed to the more favourable system. The argument that the distinction is necessary for investment subsidies to be paid via the tax system is equally unpersuasive. These do not have to be given in the form of tax remission, and even where they are, neither equity nor efficiency demands that they be restricted to those who are investing out of retained profits.

It is often maintained that there are two nations of tax-payers, those who are taxed under Schedule D and those who fall under Schedule E; among those who are taxed under the latter schedule there are two sub-nations: those with and those without fringe benefits in the form of houses or cars. There is, no doubt, a possible source of inequity here and in the United Kingdom it is doubtful whether the Schedule E rules are drawn tightly enough to prevent abuse; it is possible that the equitable solution is to give a separate flat-rate expenses allowance under Schedule E only and to increase rates payable under all schedules to make good the loss of revenue. There is, of course, a separate question of the extent of evasion under each schedule.

The proposals made so far may have a revolutionary ring about them, especially if one comes to them fresh from reading the recent White Paper on the reform of the personal direct taxation (Cmnd. 4653, 1971). None of them is new; most have a long and in many cases distinguished history and many have recently been endorsed by the Carter Commission on the Canadian tax system. Unfortunately the Carter proposals have received little attention in this country, despite the acclamation with which they were received by public finance specialists in North America. It is true that to follow this line of thinking entails far-reaching reforms. It is also true that over a period of 10 or 15 years during which such changes could be made, an equivalent expenditure of effort and energy could be devoted to making minor changes in the present system (some of this effort and energy is of course already committed to the value-added tax) the consequences of which for economic and social welfare are hardly likely to be dramatic. It is trite but true that if one goes in for tax reform one should get the best value for money that is going: no set of reforms is worth having when its cost is losing a better set.

It is naturally difficult among mortal people and quinquennial governments to summon enthusiasm for long-run changes. Yet to ignore the long run is to imperil our grandchildren. There is too little awareness of the precarious nature of our economic institutions. The British tax system is imposed on a structure of economic relationships which includes a wage system. It is taken for granted that most people will be able to earn from the sale of their labour services enough to support themselves and their families at an acceptable level. This belief has already been breached and the family income supplement, even though it may be thought a mouse of a scheme, is an historic mouse. But the situation in which a man is healthy and fit and employed, yet unable to earn enough for his own and his family's basic needs is still regarded as exceptional. It is really rather optimistic to suppose that one can rely on this continuing and that a high level of employment at high real wages can always be achieved. There is no difficulty in imagining a situation where this would not be possible.

7

The Reform of Wealth Taxes in Britain

A. B. ATKINSON[*]

In discussion of tax reform, it is rather surprising that taxes on wealth usually receive less attention than taxes on income. All the evidence suggests that wealth in Britain is much more unequally distributed than income, and the taxation of wealth offers the possibility of achieving greater equity without the adverse effects on incentives commonly supposed to be associated with income taxation. In this article, I examine the scope for reform of wealth taxation in Britain, considering the most effective way of reducing inequality and the possible disadvantages such as increased administrative costs or an adverse effect on the incentives to work and save.[1]

Concentration of Wealth in Britain

It may be useful to begin by presenting the evidence about the concentration of wealth-holding and the factors responsible for the persistence of inequality. Most of our information about the distribution of wealth comes from the estate duty returns, and for 1968 these show that the top 1 per cent of adult wealth-holders own a third of total personal wealth and the top 10 per cent nearly three quarters.[2] Although we cannot estimate from this source the number of millionaires in Britain, there are 20,000

[*] The author is Professor of Economics at the University of Essex. He has written *Poverty in Britain and the Reform of Social Security*.

1. Much of the material in this article is drawn from *Unequal Shares - Wealth in Britain*, Allen Lane The Penguin Press, 1972, which contains more detailed discussion of many of the points covered here.

2. These figures were calculated from the estimates of the Inland Revenue, *Inland Revenue Statistics 1970*, HMSO, 1970.

people with an average of some £400,000 each – an amount which it would take the average worker 300 years to earn. Moreover, the concentration of wealth-holding is far greater than that in the distribution of income before tax: the share of the top 10 per cent of income receivers is less than 30 per cent of total income. It is interesting to examine the changes in the degree of concentration of wealth-holding over time. J. R. S. Revell has compiled the following figures on a broadly comparable basis for the period 1911–60[8]:

Share of top	1%	5%	10%	of adult population
1911–13	69%	87%	92%	
1924–30	62%	84%	91%	
1936–8	56%	79%	88%	
1954	43%	71%	79%	
1960	42%	75%	83%	

This suggests a reduction in inequality over the course of this century, but there are two qualifications that should be borne in mind. The figures for any single year are subject to considerable error (since they are based on a small sample and are sensitive to chance variations), so that small changes from year to year cannot be treated as very significant. Secondly, while the share of the top 1 per cent has fallen markedly since 1911, that of the top 10 per cent has been reduced by considerably less, so that a major part of the redistribution has been from the very rich to the rich: the share of the top 1 per cent has fallen by 27 per cent, but that of the next 9 per cent has *risen* from 23 per cent (= 92 per cent –69 per cent) in 1911–13 to 41 per cent (= 83 per cent –42 per cent) in 1960.

These estimates of the distribution of wealth have a number of

3. J. R. S. Revell, 'Changes in the Social Distribution of Property in Britain During the Twentieth Century', *Actes du Troisième Congrès International d'Histoire Économique*, Vol. I, Munich, 1965. These figures are estimated using a different method from those for 1968 given above and relate to England and Wales only.

shortcomings. First, there is a large amount of wealth 'missing' from the estate duty returns: small estates for which probate is not required, pension rights and annuities and property held in trust. Some of these omissions are likely to cause the degree of inequality to be overstated, and an estimate allowing for 'missing' wealth (including the rights to state pensions) shows the share of the top 1 per cent as being about a quarter and that of the top 10 per cent over half the total personal wealth.[4] Even with this adjustment, it is clear that the degree of inequality remains very substantial. Secondly, there are good reasons for arguing that we should be concerned not with the distribution of wealth that people currently own (which is what the estate duty-based estimates show) but with the distribution of *inherited wealth* – or the amount that people receive in the form of bequests and gifts in the course of their lives. It is possible that part of the observed inequality may be due to people accumulating wealth over their lifetimes (to provide, say, for retirement) rather than to inheritance; and if the top 1 per cent hold more than their share simply because they are older and have saved more for their old age, we should not be anything like so concerned about inequality.

We do not have any direct evidence about the degree of inequality in inherited wealth, but there are two considerations which suggest that it may be substantial. Examination of the distribution of wealth among people of the same age (which should eliminate the major life-cycle differences) shows that there is still a very marked degree of concentration: the share of the top 1 per cent or 5 per cent is very similar to that for the distribution as a whole.[5] Similarly, the studies of J. Wedgwood and C. D. Harbury showed that a high proportion of those leaving large estates had fathers who themselves had left substantial

4. See A. B. Atkinson, 'The Distribution of Wealth and the Individual Life-Cycle', *Oxford Economic Papers*, 1971. As is explained in this article, this estimate is subject to a number of qualifications. It must also be remembered that some of these assets (for example, rights to state or occupational pensions) convey little or no *control* over wealth.

5. cf. 'The Distribution of Wealth and the Individual Life-Cycle', op. cit.

amounts.[6] To quote the conclusion reached by Harbury (relating to 1956–7), 'the chance of leaving an estate valued at over £100,000, or even £50,000, was outstandingly enhanced if one's father had been at least moderately well off'. This evidence is not conclusive, but indicates that there is considerable concentration in the distribution of inherited wealth and that inheritance is a major factor.

Impact of Estate Duty

The present estate duty involves very high rates of tax on the transfer of wealth at death (the nominal rate on an estate of £1 million is 75 per cent) and may thus be expected to have a major equalizing effect. However, as is well known, there are a number of ways in which property may be passed from generation to generation without duty being paid at these high rates. Although the budgets of 1968 and 1969 closed a number of loopholes, it remains possible for property to avoid tax altogether if passed on more than 7 years before death, and for the tax to be substantially reduced through the use of discretionary trusts (if properly managed) or through the concessions for timber and agricultural land. This combination of high apparent tax rates and clear avenues for avoidance recalls what the Chicago economist Henry Simons said of the American tax system:

> The whole procedure involves a subtle kind of moral and political dishonesty. One senses here a grand scheme of deception whereby enormous surtaxes are voted in exchange for promises that they will not be made effective. Thus the politicians may point with pride to the rates, while reminding their wealthy constituents of the loopholes.

Whatever one's views about the desirability of redistribution, this kind of deception cannot be regarded as an equitable basis for our system of wealth taxation.

It has sometimes been argued that the decline in inequality in the distribution of wealth since the beginning of this century is

6. J. Wedgwood, *The Economics of Inheritance*, 1929; C. D. Harbury, 'Inheritance and the Distribution of Personal Wealth', *Economic Journal*, 1962.

evidence that estate duty, despite the loopholes, has been a powerful equalizing force. However, since we have little idea what would have happened in the absence of the duty, it is not possible to make any such deduction: the decline in the share of the top 1 per cent may be due to quite independent factors. Moreover, as Revell has pointed out, the observed changes are consistent with an alternative explanation – that estate duty has led not to greater equality but simply to families passing on their wealth earlier to avoid tax. Insofar as fathers now pass on their wealth well before they die in order to avoid duty, we should observe a fall in their share (the top 1 per cent) but little change in that of the top 10 per cent (in which the sons are assumed to be included). The apparent decline in inequality may therefore be attributable to a rearrangement of wealth within families rather than any genuine redistribution of inherited wealth.

Comparison with other Countries

It is interesting to compare the concentration of wealth-holding in Britain with that in the United States. One might well expect the home of the Rockefellers, the Carnegies and the Morgans to exhibit at least as much inequality as Britain, but this is far from the case. Estimates for 1954 show that the share of the top 1 per cent in total wealth was 24 per cent in the United States compared with a corresponding figure for Britain of 43 per cent.[7] The evidence for other advanced industrial countries shows a similar picture, and it seems likely that Britain has the doubtful distinction of leading the international inequality league.

This finding is not perhaps surprising when one considers the taxes on wealth in force in the different countries. This is especially striking in the treatment of gifts *inter vivos*. The major countries with estate taxes – such as the United States, Australia and Canada – couple them with a tax on gifts to prevent avoidance: in the United States, for example, gifts are taxed at three quarters of the estate tax rates. The Scandinavian countries not

7. R. J. Lampman, *The Share of Top Wealth-holders in National Wealth 1922–1956*, National Bureau for Economic Research, 1962.

only have taxes on the transfer of wealth, but also operate annual taxes on wealth. Sweden has a successions tax on bequests, linked with a gifts tax, and a tax on net worth in excess of SKr 100,000 (about £8,000) at rates varying between 0.8 and 1.8 per cent.

Strategy for Wealth Tax Reform

Before plunging into the details of particular schemes, we should discuss certain general questions of strategy. The most important issue concerns the choice between taxing the *holding of wealth* and taxing the *transfer of wealth*. In terms of actual taxes this represents the choice between introducing an annual wealth tax and reforming our system of wealth transfer taxation. Under the former a person would pay (say) $1\frac{1}{2}$ per cent every year on the value of his wealth above a certain exemption level; under the latter, tax would be paid only when the wealth was transferred to someone else in the form of a gift or bequest. A number of factors enter into the choice between these two types of taxation and there is not scope to discuss the issue fully here; however, two considerations point clearly in the direction of favouring reform of wealth transfer taxation rather than the introduction of an annual wealth tax.

The first important consideration is the equity objective of the tax reform. As I have argued earlier, we are likely to be primarily concerned with achieving greater equality in the distribution of *inherited wealth*, and for this purpose the annual wealth tax is less suitable than wealth transfer taxation. An annual wealth tax would fall on all wealth (above the exemption level) regardless of whether it had been inherited or whether the person had saved it out of his earnings. The amount of tax that a person paid would depend on how he decided to arrange his consumption over his lifetime; and two people with the same inherited wealth would pay different amounts of tax if one saved it for his old age and the other did not. A tax levied on the transfer of wealth, on the other hand, would be directed specifically at the distribution of inherited wealth, and the amount of tax paid would not be influenced by the amount that a person had saved during his lifetime (unless he passed it on to his heirs). Adopting this form of taxation would also serve the purpose of making quite transparent the equity objective of the reform, which seems likely to increase its public acceptability.

The second consideration is one that economists are often accused of neglecting: the administrative problems of tax reform. These have commonly been put forward as an objection to the introduction of a wealth tax, and although often exaggerated (wealth taxes have been operated successfully in a number of European countries for a long time) the cost of administering the wealth tax might be substantial. With an exemption limit as high as £50,000, the Inland Revenue would still have to deal with some 200,000 wealth tax returns a year, and the amount of wealth involved would be over ten times that at present handled under estate duty. G. S. A. Wheatcroft estimated in 1964 that the administrative cost of a wealth tax with an exemption level of £25,000 would be some 13 per cent of the revenue, which is very much higher than the corresponding figure for income tax (1.5 per cent) and makes no allowance for the costs of the taxpayers.[8] A reform of wealth *transfer* taxation would also involve increased administrative costs, but it seems unlikely that they would be anything like as large, since wealth would only have to be valued once a generation rather than once a year.

There are, therefore, good grounds for preferring a reform of wealth transfer taxation to an annual wealth tax, and in what follows I concentrate on the former. There are, however, a bewildering variety of ways in which the system of taxing wealth transfers could be reformed, and we have to make at least two major decisions about the form which a new wealth transfer tax should take:

1. Should it be based on the amount *passed on* or the amount *received*? Although the first principle is that adopted with the present estate duty, it is a less effective way of achieving greater equality in the distribution of inherited wealth than a tax on

8. G. S. A. Wheatcroft, 'The Administrative Problems of a Wealth Tax', *British Tax Review*, 1963.

the amount received. In the latter case there is a definite incentive for donors to spread their wealth widely: £1 million left to 100 people would pay much less tax (assuming that the tax would be progressive) than if it were all left to a single heir, whereas with estate duty the tax would be the same.

2. Should the tax be operated on an *annual assessment period* or should it be cumulative over a person's *lifetime*? In other words, should we tax a person separately on gifts and bequests received in each tax year or should he be taxed on the grand total over his life? The argument for annual assessment is chiefly one of administrative convenience, but against that must be set the fact that it is less well suited to our equity objectives. With an annual assessment, a person receiving a succession of small gifts would pay very much less tax than on a single gift of the same total amount, which would not be equitable in terms of the distribution of inherited wealth.

The reform of wealth transfer taxation that I would favour, therefore, is the replacement of estate duty by a progressive tax on a person's total capital receipts over the course of his lifetime (bequests, gifts, etc.), and this is discussed in the next section. If this reform were felt to represent too great a departure from the existing tax system, an alternative would be the extension of the present estate duty to cover all gifts (and not just those made within seven years of death). Although this would not provide an incentive for donors to divide their wealth, it would substantially reduce the possibilities for avoidance and lead to greater equality of wealth-holding.

A Lifetime Capital-Receipts Tax

Proposals for a tax of this type have been made by J. E. Meade, C. T. Sandford and O. Stutchbury (who refers to it as a 'gratuitous enrichment tax').[9] The way in which the tax would work has been described by Meade as follows:

9. J. E. Meade, *Efficiency, Equality and the Ownership of Property,* Allen and Unwin, 1964; C. T. Sandford, *Taxing Inheritance and Capital Gains,* Hobart Paper 32; O. Stutchbury, *The Case for Capital Taxes,* Fabian Tract 388.

Every gift or legacy received by any one individual would be recorded in a register against his name for tax purposes. He would then be taxed when he received any gift or bequest according to the . . . total amount which he had received over the whole of his life by way of gift or inheritance. The rate of tax would be on a progressive scale according to the total of gifts or bequests recorded against his name in the tax register.

Meade envisaged that the tax would be levied on gifts and bequests only, but the other two authors would like to include other capital receipts: Sandford, for example, would include capital gains (abolishing the present taxes), gambling winnings and 'golden handshakes'. In what follows I assume that the tax would apply to gifts, bequests and gambling winnings.[10]

The rates proposed for the lifetime capital-receipts tax have in all cases been highly progressive, and a typical scale is shown below:

Total lifetime receipts	Marginal rate	Average rate*
less than £10,000	0	0
£10,000–£20,000	30	0
£20,000–£30,000	40	15
£30,000–£50,000	50	23
£50,000–£100,000	75	34
£100,000–£200,000	80	55
£200,000 and above	85	70

*At the lower end of the range.

The second column shows the *marginal* rate of tax – or the rate applied to each extra £1 received in that range – and the third column shows the *average* rate payable on the whole amount at the lower end of the bracket. A man who had received a total of £50,000 would have paid 34 per cent of it in tax, and would pay tax at the rate of 75 per cent on the next £50,000 he got. The fact that the tax is levied on the amount received rather than the

10. Two important points not discussed here are the treatment of discretionary and other trusts, and the definition of the tax-paying unit.

estate left means that the revenue would tend to be lower than with a corresponding estate duty (since in many cases estates are divided between several heirs and the proposed tax provides a much increased incentive to do so). However, the rates of tax are higher than the present estate duty and gifts *inter vivos* now escaping tax and gambling winnings would be included. The net revenue may therefore be little different from that of the estate duty or even higher.

What would be the impact of the lifetime capital-receipts tax on the distribution of inherited wealth? It is clear that it would provide a powerful incentive for people to spread their wealth more widely. If a person leaves £30,000 to a man who has already received £200,000, the net amount passed on after tax is only £4,500; but the same amount left to a person who had inherited nothing would give a net bequest of £23,000. Although the precise extent of the equalizing effect cannot be estimated, there can be little doubt that the lifetime capital-receipts tax would be much more effective than the present estate duty in reducing inequality (if only because it would catch the gifts that now avoid taxation).

The Arguments Against

The principal arguments made against any reform of wealth taxation is that it would discourage savings, enterprise or work effort. It is important, therefore, to examine whether the replacement of estate duty by a lifetime capital-receipts tax would have adverse effects of this kind.

It has been argued that passing on wealth to one's children is an important motive for saving among the wealthy and that more effective taxes on the transfer of wealth could therefore be expected to lead to a fall in savings. However, it does not necessarily follow that the tax would discourage saving. Suppose that a person aimed to pass on to his son the amount he himself had inherited. If a tax on the transfer of wealth is introduced, he would then save *more* to make up for the amount paid in tax. Moreover, even if it were true that potential donors did save less, this represents only part of the picture and we have to examine also the reactions of the recipients. If a person has reduced expectations of an inheritance, he may well increase his saving: an increase in grandfather's consumption as a result of the tax being a signal for his own retrenchment. It should also be remembered that there would not be the same incentive as under estate duty to pass wealth on early and the transmission of wealth is likely to be delayed, which means that heirs would face greater uncertainty about the amount they will inherit and the date at which they will receive it. Without the security of having their inheritance safely in their pocket, they may be expected to save more themselves.

A further objection sometimes put forward is that the extension of wealth transfer taxation would lead to people taking their wealth out of the country – the 'standing room only in the Bahamas' argument. The force of this objection is, however, reduced by the fact that other countries have managed to introduce substantial wealth taxes without such a capital flight apparently taking place; and allowance must be made for the growing political risk that present tax 'havens' may become less favourably disposed towards immigrant capital.

The argument with regard to work effort and enterprise is similar – that people work in order to save and that they save in order to pass wealth on. Again, this ignores the effect on the recipients and if the lifetime capital-receipts tax leads to a reduction in the amount of wealth passed on, this can be expected to increase the incentive to work of the heirs with diminished 'expectations'. Alfred Nobel is reported to have said:

> I regard large inherited wealth as a misfortune which merely serves to dull men's faculties ... I consider it a mistake to hand over to children considerable sums of money. To do so merely encourages laziness.

Conclusions

The distribution of wealth in Britain is extremely unequal – much more so than in most other advanced industrial countries – and there is no clear evidence of a rapid reduction in inequality over time. The present estate duty gives the appearance of high rates of taxation but there are still straightforward methods for avoidance; and this 'deception' cannot be regarded as an equitable basis for wealth taxation. These factors suggest a clear need for the reform of wealth taxes in Britain.

Such a reform could take a number of different forms. The introduction of an annual wealth tax or the supplementation of estate duty by a tax on gifts would certainly help bring about greater equality. I have argued, however, that there are a number of reasons for preferring a lifetime capital-receipts tax: it would be more successful in meeting our equity objectives of taxing inherited wealth, it would make transparent the underlying principle of taxation, and it would not involve the same administrative problems as an annual wealth tax. The objections most commonly raised to a reform of this kind (that it would discourage savings or work effort) have been shown to be based on an incomplete analysis of its likely effects, and it is quite possible that it would have the reverse effect. The introduction of a lifetime capital-receipts tax may in fact offer us the opportunity of achieving greater equity without the disincentive effects which many people believe to be associated with progressive income taxation.

8
Death Duties

CEDRIC SANDFORD*

Death duties are among the most popular – or least unpopular –
of taxes with governments and, if governments can be presumed
to reflect the wishes of the governed, with citizens also. Almost
without exception the countries with 'mixed' economics tax
wealth transfers at death; and many have done so for centuries.
Quite apart from medieval dues on death, taxes in the United
Kingdom have an unbroken history from 1694; under Dutch
influence probate duty was then first introduced as a regressive
stamp duty. Today's highly progressive estate duty was based on
Sir William Harcourt's reform of 1894.

Because of their extensive history, spatially and temporally,
because of the varied forms death duties may take and not least
because they affect the basic social and economic structure of a
society – the distribution of wealth and the institution of inheritance – a study of the history of death duties throws fascinating lights on contemporary society: the pressures of fiscal
expediency, the administrative constraints in fiscal policy,
changing political philosophy, economic and social conflicts.

Why Death Duties?

This comparative popularity of death duties reflects the dis-
tinctive merits of death taxation. If income is the best *single*
criterion of 'ability to pay' (whatever definition is given to that
elusive yardstick), the equity of the tax system is increased if

*The author is Professor of Political Economy and Head of the School of
Humanities and Social Sciences at the University of Bath. He has
written *Taxing Inheritance and Capital Gains*, Institute of Economic Affairs,
Taxation, and *Taxing Personal Wealth*, Allen & Unwin.

income tax is supplemented by a wealth tax. In this way allowance is made for the taxable capacity which wealth confers on its possessor over and above the income (if any) derived from it – a taxable capacity based on the advantages of security and opportunity which ownership of wealth brings. And the most convenient of all wealth taxes is a death duty.

Wealth taxes all suffer from the big administrative disadvantage of difficulties of valuation; but with death duties, valuation problems are minimized; the total amount of property to be valued in any one year for death duties is only a small proportion, perhaps one fortieth, of the total of personal wealth. Thus the valuation problems can more easily be encompassed and also the effect on the market values of assets sold to meet death duties is slight as compared with, say, the problems of a once-and-for-all capital levy. Moreover, the tax is imposed at a time when an inventory of property and probably a valuation is required anyway to carry out the will of the deceased or implement the law of intestacy.

Further, if the intention behind the death duties is to diminish inequalities of wealth – which is certainly true of many modern duties, though not of their antecedents – death duties can perform this function with less tax-payer hostility and less economic disturbance than any alternative tax so heavy as of necessity to be met from capital – such as a capital levy during the lifetime of the property owner, or a heavy annual capital tax.

Death duties at current high rates necessarily reduce the total of private saving, but this can be made good by the state using the revenue from death duties for debt redemption; or, at any rate, not treating it as ordinary revenue for current expenditure. We must recognize our ignorance of the effect of death duties on the *incentive* to save; but they do not *necessarily* reduce it: a desire to bequeath is only one of many motives for saving and the other motives are unaffected by death duties. Moreover, death duties may stimulate some property owners with a strong desire to bequeath to save *more* – in order to hand on to subsequent generations as large a net of tax estate as possible – as well as discouraging some others from saving. In anticipation of the effect of tax in reducing a legacy, prospective heirs may also be more willing to save than if there were no death duty. Death duties have little or no effect on the incentive to effort where the purpose of the effort is consumption rather than saving; and similarly with enterprise in general – although there are particular problems in connection with family businesses in agriculture and industry.

Another special merit can be claimed for death duties. Many would hold that there is a particular moral justification for taxing *inherited* wealth, i.e. wealth which, in general, is unrelated to the effort of those who benefit by it.

These are very real merits; yet death duties suffer from defects which in practice create what C. Lowell Harris has conveniently, if vaguely, called 'injustices'.[1] These injustices are partly inherent in death duties. Because the circumstance giving rise to death duty liability is not a market transaction, like the sale of a product or factor of production, there is no market value which can be taken as the equivalent of worth between buyer and seller. Hence, there is an element of arbitrariness in the determination of 'market values'. The concept of a death duty as levied on 'property passing at death' is far too simple: gifts have to be taken into account and also trusts and settlements where income rights may alter as a result of a death, even if no wealth changes hands. To meet such circumstances the tax becomes complex and loses objectivity; and trusts and gifts also offer loopholes for avoidance. Finally, whilst the fact of death is certain, the time is uncertain; hence planning to meet the tax, or to avoid it, becomes something of a gamble, with corresponding inequities.

The conclusion to be drawn is that, whilst death duties have substantial merits, the possible sources of injustice point the need to choose a form of death duty appropriate to its purpose; to apply much thought and care in devising administrative arrangements to minimize the defects of the tax; and perhaps also to exercise some circumspection about how high rates of death

1. 'Sources of Injustice in Death Taxation', *National Tax Journal*, December 1954.

duty should be pushed, because the higher the rates the more serious are the inequities likely to be and the more active the search for measures of avoidance.

Forms of Death Taxation

At this point we must define our terms. In this article we use death duty or death taxation to cover any form of tax on wealth transfers arising from a death (or in anticipation of death). Death taxes have many variants but two major species can be distinguished – estate duty and inheritance tax (or legacy or succession duties). An estate duty is a death duty levied on the total net property left by the deceased, irrespective of how that property is to be distributed under the terms of the will or the laws of intestacy. An inheritance tax, on the other hand, is a tax levied on what is received by heirs regardless of the size of the estate from which it comes. The inheritance tax especially lends itself to variants. The simplest form of inheritance tax is one in which the beneficiary is taxed independently on each bequest received. A second form is to tax on the cumulative aggregate received in bequests over a period of years or even over a lifetime. A third variant is to relate inheritance tax not only to the size of the bequest but also to the existing wealth of the beneficiary. A very common feature of inheritance taxes, typical of most European taxes, is graduation not only according to the size of individual bequests but also according to the closeness of the relationship between beneficiary and deceased, so that near relatives pay tax on a lower scale than distant relatives or strangers in blood.

The relative merits of estate duty and inheritance tax have been the subject of historical controversy and remain a matter of dispute today. When Sir William Harcourt introduced his estate duty of 1894, the first *consistently* progressive tax in British history, the main debate in the House of Commons took place around two issues: the principle of graduation or progression, and the *form* a reformed death duty should take. The Conservative Opposition would have preferred the inheritance tax form. Additional point was given to the dispute by the publication after his death of Lord Randolph Churchill's budget proposals,[2] prepared for 1886 but never introduced, to replace all existing death duties by a single graduated inheritance tax.

What then are the arguments for and against these two kinds of death duty? They may be considered under four heads: incidence and equity; equality; revenue; and administration.

Incidence and Equity

Harcourt justified the estate duty form of tax in 1894 by several arguments which implied that the incidence of the tax was on the deceased. First he propounded the spurious legal argument that because the rights a man had to dispose of property after his death were conferred by law, then the state, as guardian of the law, had the *prior* right to a share in the property – and this *first* claim logically implied the estate duty form of tax. More serious consideration should be given to his contention that estate duty was a 'back tax' in lieu of income tax on the deceased. At the time it was held to be administratively impracticable both to introduce progression into the income tax, and also differentiate between sources of income so that income from work paid at a lower rate than income from property (which was more permanent and secure and not dependent on the life and health of a particular person). A progressive estate duty, Harcourt maintained, compensated for these deficiencies in the income tax.

Whatever the contemporary validity of his arguments, since Harcourt's day progression and differentiation have both been introduced into income tax. Since then, death duties have become so heavy that there is now little likelihood of a property owner, by insurance or other means, attempting to save against the duty. Thus, as Professor Nicholas Kaldor has put it:[3]

Death duty is a periodic levy on property falling on the person or persons who inherit a man's estate. The legal notion that estate duty is

2. Winston S. Churchill, *Lord Randolph Churchill*, Macmillan, 1906, Chaps. 15 and 16.

3. N. Kaldor, 'The Reform of Personal Taxation', *Essays on Economic Policy*, Vol. I, Duckworth, 1964, pp. 212–13.

a tax on the deceased is really nonsensical – though it may have had rather more justification in the old days when people saved during their lifetime to cover death duty liabilities on their decease. If the incidence of estate duty is really on the legatee and not on the testator, the sensible thing is to recognize this and to impose a tax on the recipient.

Or, as Winston Churchill pungently expressed it, we should 'tax the living instead of trying to tax the dead'.[4] Only if death duty takes the form of an inheritance tax can it be related to the economic circumstances of the beneficiaries – i.e., in some sense levied according to 'ability to pay'.

Equality

In the debates of 1894 the argument that death duties should be used to diminish inequalities of wealth played a minor part, although it was to some extent implicit in the adoption of progressive rates (1 per cent rising to a maximum of 8 per cent of the total estate). Since then the maximum rate of duty has risen tenfold in nominal terms and more in real terms when allowance is made for inflation, as a result of which an estate of a particular size in real terms is assimilated into ever higher tax brackets. Death duties at this level do little or nothing to reduce current demand for goods and services (the prime purpose of taxation in general); rather they are concerned essentially with the distribution of assets both between the public and private sectors and within the private sector. If this is so, then either there is little point in imposing death duties *or* their purpose is to be found in their effect on the distribution of wealth – e.g., in reducing inequality. It is the second view which the author supports, although the issue is essentially one of personal value-judgement. But if the prime purpose of death duties *is* to reduce inequalities of wealth, then the form of duty chosen ought to be that most effective for the purpose, subject only to constraints such as a humane concern for widows and dependent children and the need to guard against adverse economic effects.

4. ibid.

There are two reasons for believing that an inheritance tax would be more effective than estate duty in reducing wealth in-equality. First, it is large inheritances, not large estates as such, that *perpetuate* inequality; an estate of £200,000 left to one heir results in bigger inequalities than an estate of £1 million equally divided amongst a hundred heirs. A tax graduated in relation to the size of the inheritance thus strikes at the heart of the problem. Further, the inheritance tax offers an incentive to spread wealth more widely, because the more a property owner spreads his bequests, the less the total tax paid on them. How important this inducement is we do not know; where there are surviving spouses and children it may have little influence, but in other cases it is possible that the incentive to disperse may be effective.

Revenue

Consideration of the dispersal of estates brings us naturally to one of the main contentions used by Harcourt and others to support estate duty, i.e., that it is a better revenue-yielder than inheritance tax. This is obviously true if we compare an estate duty and a legacy duty with the same nominal rates of tax; then only if an estate were left to a single heir would the inheritance tax yield the same revenue as estate duty; but in all other cases the yield would be less. For instance, in round terms and ignoring special concessions, at present rates estate duty on £1 million is about 80 per cent (average) and on an estate of £100,000 about 50 per cent (average). Thus, under estate duty, if a man dies leaving £1 million, tax paid is £800,000 however the estate is distributed. Under inheritance tax with the same nominal rates, revenue re-ceived by the Exchequer is only as much as this if the estate is left to a single heir. If, for example, it were equally divided amongst 10 people, £100,000 each, then under inheritance tax the total revenue to the Exchequer would be £500,000, a short-fall of £300,000. But the rates of inheritance tax do not *need* to be the same as estate duty; a structure of rates could be designed to raise approximately the same revenue; then estates left to single heirs would pay more, estates widely dispersed would pay less.

This raises a significant issue, however. Does it matter if the revenue falls? As we have said, death duties do not fulfil the same purpose as taxes in general, in that they do little or nothing to reduce current demand for resources. If the purpose of the death duties is to reduce inequalities of wealth, is not the yield of the tax beside the point? The answer is 'Not entirely'. An inheritance tax might be expected to reduce inequalities in two ways. (i) It would provide some incentive for wide diffusion of property and, insofar as this happened, the tax objective could be achieved with a reduction in revenue. (Thus, to illustrate by a hypothetical extreme, if all estate owners distributed estates in such small 'parcels' that their bequests all fell below the exemption limit, then the tax would yield no revenue, but would have achieved its objective admirably.) (ii) The other, and perhaps more likely, way in which inheritance tax reduces inequality is by taxing with particular severity the large inheritance; this method of reducing inequality *is* related to revenue received; and the larger the proportion of big inheritances taken in tax, the more likely is there to be a move towards equality. Perhaps, if one substituted inheritance tax for estate duty, the course of practical wisdom would be to devise a rate structure from which, on the basis of the existing pattern of property dispersal at death, the same total revenue might be expected initially. One would anticipate, however, that as the duty proved more effective in diminishing inequality of wealth, there would subsequently be a fall in total revenue compared with the yield if estate duty had remained. What is important is to recognize that the criterion by which to judge the tax is its effect on the distribution of wealth rather than its revenue yield.

Administration

Perhaps the strongest of the general arguments for estate duty as against inheritance tax is administrative; an estate duty requires one account and one rate of duty for each estate. Even the simplest form of inheritance tax requires more than one account save in the exceptional case of an estate left to one heir, and generally more than one rate of duty. However, in practice the administrative advantage is not so clearly on the side of estate duty. For the practical choice is not between estate duty and inheritance tax on their own but, at the least between estate duty integrated with a gifts tax and inheritance tax integrated with a gifts tax – for we shall argue below that a comprehensive gifts tax is essential to check avoidance. There is no doubt that a gifts tax can be much more readily integrated with inheritance tax than with estate duty. Under inheritance tax, gifts and inheritances can be treated precisely on a par, with gifts tax being paid by the donee just as inheritance tax is paid by the legatee. Under estate duty, gifts cannot readily be treated as though they were bequests because the appropriate rate of duty will not be known until the donor dies.[5]

Reforming Britain's Estate Duty

International comparisons of taxation are notoriously difficult, and comparisons of death duties are complicated by differences of legal systems, death duty forms, exemption provisions, consanguinity scales, special concessions, even differences in valuation principles and practice; but there can be no doubt that the *nominal* rates of death duty in the United Kingdom (set out in the Table opposite) are markedly higher than those of most other 'mixed' economies and may well rank as the highest in the world.

If the United Kingdom has possibly the highest death duty rates of any comparable country, it also has the doubtful distinction that its estate duty is amongst the easiest to avoid. Most serious students of the estate duty in Britain have concluded that two interrelated reforms are essential: the rates should be reduced and at the same time be made more effective, in particular by the introduction of a comprehensive gifts tax. At present gifts count as 'realization' under the capital-gains tax, so that the donor is

5. Some of the complications to which this gives rise can be seen by examining the proposals of Professor G. S. A. Wheatcroft, *Estate Duty and Gift Taxation*, Sweet and Maxwell, 1965, pp. 126–32.

taxed on the capital gain (if any) in the gift. If a person dies within seven years after having made a gift, the gift is aggregated with the estate for assessment of estate duty; but Britain is one of the few countries which does not support its death duty with a general gifts tax. Thus, apart from more sophisticated arrangements, a simple way of death duty avoidance always remains: to give one's property away and live for seven years.

Estate Duty Rates

Slice of net capital value		Rate of duty when death occurred after 30 March 1971
Over	*Not over*	
£	£	%
—	12,500	Nil
12,500	17,500	25
17,500	30,000	30
30,000	40,000	45
40,000	80,000	60
80,000	150,000	65
150,000	300,000	70
300,000	500,000	75
500,000	750,000	80
750,000	—	85*

*With a ceiling of 80 per cent of the total estate.
Source: *Financial Statement and Budget Report 1971-72*, March 1971.

Agreed on the need to reduce death duty rates and introduce gifts tax, the reformers then part company. Professors G. S. A. Wheatcroft[6] and A. R. Prest[7] remain unconvinced of the superiority of inheritance tax and prefer to retain the estate duty form. There are always strong arguments for fiscal conservatism because introducing a new tax causes a major disruption: a

6. ibid.
7. *Public Finance in Theory and Practice*, Weidenfeld and Nicolson, 3rd ed., 1967, Chap. 15.

lengthy and difficult transition period with additional work both for revenue officers and for tax-payers and their professional advisers; it also makes obsolete the 'human capital' embodied in the skills of the tax experts. Other would-be reformers, however, believe that the benefits of the change would outweigh these costs and advocate an inheritance tax.[8] The form they most favour is that by which inheritances and gifts are taxed cumulatively over a lifetime. Administratively, a cumulative inheritance tax (which is sometimes called an accessions tax) would require the maintenance of records for each tax-payer indicating the gifts and legacies received throughout his (or her) lifetime; whilst this inevitably adds to the cost of administration, this form of inheritance tax has the merit that it would be more effective in diminishing inequality than a simple inheritance tax. And it would prevent avoidance by a property owner who made a series of gifts to the same person over a period of time, for, under this cumulative inheritance or accessions tax, the same duty would be paid on a single large legacy as on a number of smaller legacies of the same total, as shown in the following example. Suppose the (average) rate of tax on an inheritance of £100,000 was 50 per cent and that on an inheritance of £50,000 was 30 per cent. Then anyone receiving two legacies (or gifts) of £50,000 at different times would pay exactly the same as someone receiving one legacy of £100,000 – as shown in the Table on p. 123.

This cumulative inheritance tax could, if desired, be extended into a general capital-receipts tax to include all non-income receipts (long-term capital gains, gambling winnings, 'golden handshakes', as well as gifts and legacies). Then all net receipts would either be subject to income tax on an annual basis or to capital-receipts tax on a cumulative lifetime basis.

Whatever the form of a reformed death duty, there are a number of proposals for changes of detail which deserve serious

8. For example, J. E. Meade, *Efficiency, Equality and the Ownership of Property*, George Allen & Unwin, 1964; Oliver Stutchbury, *The Case for Capital Taxes*, Fabian Tract 388, December 1968; C. T. Sandford, *Taxing Inheritance and Capital Gains*, IEA, 2nd ed. 1967, and, more fully, in *Taxing Personal Wealth*, George Allen & Unwin, 1971.

	Legacies/ gifts received	Cumulative total of legacies and gifts	Tax rate	Tax paid	Cumulative total tax paid
	£	£	%	£	£
1st	50,000	50,000	30	15,000	15,000
2nd	50,000	100,000	50	35,000*	50,000

*Made up as follows:	£
£100,000 at 50 per cent	50,000
less tax already paid	15,000
tax paid on receipt of 2nd legacy	35,000

consideration. The concessionary rates to certain assets of private businesses and more especially the duty abatement on the agricultural value of agricultural property are a source of inequity and of estate duty avoidance. The agricultural concession has also helped to raise land prices and these provisions are of doubtful justification. The difficulties of small businesses and agricultural owner-occupiers are best met by the reduction in the rates of duty already suggested, and by general provisions for the payment of duty by instalments for all assets of limited marketability and divisibility. From its introduction, estate duty could be paid on real property by 8 yearly, or 16 half-yearly, instalments. In the 1971 budget the Chancellor proposed to extend this provision to unincorporated businesses, non-quoted shares valued on an 'assets basis', and leasehold property. But even this latest concession still leaves some gaps, e.g. the forced sale of a large block of shares in a private company not valued on the assets basis, or in a small public company, might cause hardship and economic problems, depressing the price to the detriment of heirs and adversely affecting the terms on which the firm can raise new capital in the future. Another proposed reform which might help with these problems, as well as providing a security for the tax-payer against over-valuation, might be the extension of the present very limited arrangements for payment in kind, so that the tax-payer could choose to hand over any assets at the estate duty valuation as part payment of duty. These assets could be managed by a commission, on behalf of the Revenue, which could sell them if and when it wished or could retain them to provide income for the Exchequer. As Professor Harry G. Johnson has pointed out, there is much to be said for allowing the government a direct share in the income which its actions have helped to create, instead of relying on tax income. 'One way of moving in this direction would be to accumulate the proceeds of inheritance taxes in the form of a government portfolio of ordinary shares and industrial bonds, instead of spending them as current income.'[9]

Finally, there is a need for special treatment of widows and dependent children, particularly if inheritance tax supersedes estate duty, for the exemption limit for individual legacies would necessarily be less under inheritance tax than the £12,500 exemption of the present estate duty. There are various ways of giving this relief, but the author particularly favours adopting an aspect of Swedish practice: unless specific arrangements are made to the contrary, under Swedish law the property of husband and wife is treated as their common property. If the marriage breaks up either by divorce or death, half the property is attributed to each partner. Thus, at the death of the husband, only half the property is liable to death duty, the other half is the property of the widow. Our new divorce law in the United Kingdom has moved rather nearer to the Swedish position; so why not a similar move in relation to property left at death? It would help both to meet a fiscal need and promote equal treatment of the sexes.

Postscript

Since this essay was written and put into print, the Chancellor has proposed, in the 1972 budget, substantial modifications to

9. Harry G. Johnson, 'The Social Policy of an Opulent Society', in *Money, Trade and Economic Growth*, George Allen & Unwin, 1962, p. 194.

estate duty. The main changes are an increase in the general exemption limit to £15,000; a special exemption of £15,000 for a surviving spouse; and a new and lower scale of rates of duty with a maximum of 75 per cent. With the budget the Government published a Green Paper to promote a discussion on the possibility of substituting some kind of inheritance tax for estate duty.

9
Taxation and Growth

ALAN R. PREST*

The very first thing we must do is to define our subject with some precision. Both the distinction between taxation and fees for collectively provided services and that between items which can alternatively be thought of as positive entries on the expenditure side or negative entries on the revenue side of the government's accounts are very thin. So we shall feel free in this paper to construe the term 'taxation' in a wide sense – including all the items (other than borrowing) usually listed on the revenue side and also the various forms of transfer payments which are conventionally entered on the expenditure side. But we shall regard government spending on goods and services ('exhaustive expenditures') as largely outside our terms of reference. The definition of 'growth' in turn raises at least three major questions. First, we shall mainly confine ourselves to the growth of Gross National Product per head, whilst recognizing that there are arguments for various alternatives, e.g., taking GNP rather than GNP per head, and taking consumption rather than GNP. There is also a further distinction between the growth rate of *actual* GNP per head (i.e., what actually happens) and that of *potential* GNP per head (i.e., what would happen if short-term deviations from trend could be eliminated). We shall need to keep both versions in mind. Secondly, it is important to be aware of the distinction between a temporary or non-recurrent change in the growth rate and a permanent one. This is a frequent source of confusion and it may be worth clarifying it by a simple

*The author has been successively lecturer in economics at Cambridge, then Professor of Economics at Manchester University, and now occupies a Chair in Economics at the London School of Economics. He has published books and articles in the field of public finance.

example of the former. Suppose that the growth rate of GNP depends entirely on the growth rate of the labour force. Then imagine a sudden dictatorial order that all housewives must take jobs within three months. During this period there would then be a sharp rise in output (ignoring any loss of housewives' services in the home) but once it was over the growth rate would revert to that permitted by the normal expansion of the labour force, which one can think of as being roughly related to that of population. Thirdly, insofar as one is considering a *permanent* change in the growth rate, one can divide the reasons for any such event into two: there may be an increase in the growth rate of productive inputs or there may be a change in the ratio of output growth to input growth. We shall make use of this distinction in our discussion of possible tax measures for growth.

In a subject as wide as taxation and growth, we must restrict the scope of the discussion if we are to avoid complete superficiality. In particular, we shall not deal with the questions raised in recent years by Dr Mishan about the undesirability of a faster rate of growth in view of the unwelcome side-effects likely to come from it; nor in any systematic way with the causes of economic growth, as set out by such writers as Edward Denison: rather we shall confine ourselves to a few selected topics – the influence of taxation on physical investment and on work and enterprise, the case for various types of selective intervention, and the role of demand management. It cannot be too strongly emphasized that this is a highly selective – and some, no doubt, will say idiosyncratic – treatment of the subject.

Influence of Taxation on Investment

It is usually argued that physical capital formation plays an important role in the growth process, even though it has become less customary in recent years to pay as much attention to this factor as was formerly the case.

In assessing the influence of taxation on physical investment, the first thing to emphasize is that in the United Kingdom the public sector (including the nationalized industries) is responsible for nearly half the total today. The exact figures naturally vary a bit from year to year[1] but roughly speaking we can say the dwellings total is shared equally between the public and private sectors, that the former is more important than the latter in other construction work, but that the reverse holds for investment in plant and vehicles. Whatever the potential effect of tax, or, for that matter, monetary policies on investment, one must therefore face the fact that only about half the total is likely to be affected by them in any straightforward way. Moreover, a large proportion of private sector investment (e.g., vehicles) is short-lived and so much less likely to be affected by policies bearing on the rate of return than if it were more durable. So whatever the possibilities of influencing investment by fiscal policies, we must recognize that we are dealing with a strictly limited part of the total. Or, putting the same point the other way round, the direct control of nationalized industry investment and the like must play an extremely important part in determining the total of investment, however hard one tries to influence the private sector by monetary or fiscal policy.

Given that tax policy is only relevant for about half of total investment, what form should it take? It is convenient to separate the *direct* from the *indirect* influences of tax policy on investment.

As far as *direct* influences go, the first proposition is that one should reduce tax rates on business enterprise in one way or another, e.g., by reducing taxes on profits or granting relief on capital investment in some way. There are many devices of the latter kind (e.g., initial allowances, investment allowances, free depreciation, investment grants), each with merits and demerits. We shall not discuss these in detail but it is worth noting one particular point: where there is a system allowing substantial relief against tax for capital investment, a cut in profits taxation can actually *reduce* investment incentives – in that the loss in value of the investment relief is greater than the gain in profits from the

1. See annual *National Income Blue Book* for details; e.g., in 1968 the public sector accounted for about 47½ per cent of domestic capital formation and in 1969 for 45½ per cent.

tax-rate cut. This proposition is not important in the UK today, but could become so if we were to have a very liberal system of investment allowances again.

A slightly less direct tax incentive for investment would be the substitution, in whole or in part, of a value-added tax or pay-roll tax for the present system of taxing business profits. A value-added tax of the type operating on the Continent exempts purchases of capital goods, along with bought-in components, from tax and so becomes, in effect, a tax exempting capital investment, i.e., it is a tax on consumption. Alternatively, it can be thought of as approximating to a tax which exempts prospective gross profits and so reduces to one on wages and salaries.[2] That is why, from this point of view, one can think of a value-added tax and a pay-roll tax as being alternatives – either of them is likely to increase the range of profitable investment, compared to a system of business profits taxation such as we have in the UK today, precisely because in one case we are taxing profits and in the other we are exempting them from tax.

The Difficulties of Measurement

The *precise* extent to which tax changes of this sort are likely to affect the level of physical investment is another matter. There has been a great deal of investigation into these matters in the USA in recent years; but little unanimity about the results. A number of inquiries of business firms in this country a few years ago seemed to indicate that tax variables played little part in their investment decisions. But there are some grounds for thinking that these answers may have been rather misleading; and a more recent study does seem to suggest a more positive role for these devices.[3] However, it is a fair summary to say that – as in many other fields of economics – we can speak with much more cer-

2. For the detailed argument, cf. C. S. Shoup, *Public Finance*, Weidenfeld & Nicolson, London, 1969, Chaps. 9 and 16.

3. cf. R. Agarwala and G. C. Goodson, 'An Analysis of the Effects of Investment Incentives on Investment Behaviour in the British Economy', *Economica*, November 1969.

tainty about the general direction of the effects than about their precise magnitude.

Quite apart from such direct effects, or potential effects, of tax changes on the level of investment, there are other *indirect* ways. It is frequently argued, for instance, that stimulation of demand by tax cuts or similar measures is a potent means of generating investment. If a firm is operating at full, or nearly full, capacity, it can only produce additional output by installing more capacity; whereas if it has surplus capacity, it can expand output by hiring more labour. Therefore, the argument runs, the best way of generating more capital investment is to ensure that existing capacity is kept at full stretch.

Evidence on this proposition is less than clear-cut. It has been maintained by some that post-war increases in private investment in the UK have been more closely associated with *increases* in output than with *high levels* of output. So while many would agree that there is an indirect role for taxation to play in this context it is by no means easy to say exactly what form it should take.

Emphasis is sometimes placed on the influence of taxation on the quality rather than the quantity of physical investment. This distinction is by no means straightforward but there is perhaps one point deserving of mention. There are grounds for arguing that a system of income taxation with very liberal provisions for offsetting losses may be more conducive to risk-bearing than a value-added tax of the European type.[4] So if an aim of policy is to give special encouragement to especially risky investments, one should perhaps be rather careful about unequivocal endorsement of the merits of value-added taxation and the like against taxes covering all forms of income.

4. If we regard the value-added tax of the Continental type as a zero tax on profits, its imposition does not reduce either the mean or the variance of the return from an investment, when expressed as a fraction of the capital contributed by the investor, i.e., there is no tax on rewards when lucky but also no compensation for losses when unlucky.

Taxation and Work Incentives

Encouragement to labour and enterprise may have many different aims in view. The volume of physical or mental effort by any single person is one; others are the numbers seeking work, the numbers willing to move from a given job or area to another and the numbers willing to undergo further education and training. In principle, tax rates may affect any or all of these; e.g., a decision whether to move from one area to another should incorporate calculations of the present value of the stream of *post-tax* rewards in alternative employments, the present value of the annual differences in living costs (if any) and the capital cost of the move. But before examining in more detail the part which taxes are likely to play in practice, we must note a rather important distinction. Even if a change in the tax system were to increase effort or reduce slackness in some sense, this could only be expected to give a temporary, and not a permanent, boost to the growth rate of GNP per head. If, taking a very crude example, people were induced to work 45 hours a week instead of 40, this would mean an immediate jump in the *level* of output but once this was achieved, the percentage growth *rate* would revert to something like the pre-existing one. On the other hand, this argument does not, or need not, hold for education and training: a permanent change in the percentage annual addition to the stock of human capital might reasonably be expected to lead to a permanently faster growth rate.

The tax policy change usually advocated in the work and enterprise context is the substitution of more indirect for direct taxation. One has to be very careful here. In principle, it is perfectly possible to set up a system of taxes on goods and services with exactly the same incentive/disincentive effects as arise with a system of taxing incomes. In practice, we commonly find important differences and, in particular, higher marginal tax rates in the latter case. But even so, we must face the fact that, of the many inquiries made into work attitudes in this country and elsewhere, none (to my knowledge at any rate) has yet demonstrated conclusively that high marginal rates are an important deterrent to work. There are a number of reasons – not least the current trends in Canada and the USA – why the present structure of marginal rates of income tax and surtax in this country cannot be defended, but we should delude ourselves if we thought there was as yet any firm and conclusive evidence that the crude work-incentives argument is one of them.

There are some alternative ideas in this field to which too little attention has been paid. These centre around the proposition that tax remissions should be attached to increases in income or output. One suggestion is that if we had a general value-added tax, the amounts of tax actually payable by a firm should be proportional to the amount of value added in a year but also inversely related to the *increment* in value added between one year and the next. There are all sorts of snags to overcome in any such proposal,[5] but it does at least have the merits of providing a most direct link between reward and achievement. Another suggestion is that the tax treatment of stock options given to executives could be improved with advantage. It is well known that the UK tax law is a good deal less generous in this field than is found in many countries.

It is not a modern discovery that selective intervention by government may be a means of raising the growth rate. Tariffs were a means of encouraging growth in the nineteenth century, especially in the USA and Germany; and Marshall's *Principles of Economics*, published in 1890, contained the famous proposal for taxing diminishing returns and subsidizing increasing-returns industries. But some of the manifestations of the general idea are very modern. We shall illustrate three of them here: the differential taxation of industries; of regions; and a tax proposal relating to the balance of payments.

5. cf. A. R. Prest, 'Sense and Nonsense in Budgetary Policy', *Economic Journal*, March 1968, for a review of the literature and the associated problems.

Discriminatory Taxes

The best-known example of the first is selective employment tax (SET), which in effect taxes services and the like at a much higher rate than manufacturing industry. The rationale of this tax would seem to be closely linked with Professor Kaldor's well-known arguments about the reasons for the slow growth of the UK[6] – in a nutshell, that a fast rate of growth of manufacturing output is necessary to obtain a fast rate of growth of GNP, that the former is restricted by the availability of labour and that the tax system can play a role in prising labour out of unproductive services into the vital manufacturing sector. Arguments are likely to rage for some time to come both on the credibility of this hypothesis and on the merits of a differential employment tax. The general explanatory power of increasing-returns arguments is indeed great in the growth context; but whether they are the whole or even a substantial part of the truth in the particular case of the UK is another matter. And although there is some evidence that SET may have improved productivity in some industries, especially the distributive trades, there are various counter-arguments, such as the anomalies and inefficiencies resulting from attempts to draw lines between 'worthy' and 'unworthy' activities. The general verdict must be that although a case can be made in principle for differential treatment of industries, the most celebrated example of it in this country in modern times has not been an unqualified success.

The principal growth argument (there are, of course, others) for regional fiscal intervention is associated with the pressure of overall demand. It is argued that there is a non-linear relation between the rate of rise of wages and the pressure of demand. Therefore, if a particular level of aggregate demand is oriented towards development areas, it may be associated with a slower rate of rise of wages than one which is not; alternatively, one can have a higher pressure of demand but without any faster rise in wages in the former case and this can be deemed to have

6. cf. *The Causes of the Slow Rate of Economic Growth of the UK*, Cambridge University Press, 1966.

beneficial consequences for growth. Hence the arguments for special labour and capital incentives in the outer regions of the UK. Once again, we have an example of a proposition which, even though it be valid in general principle, is hard to implement without unwanted side-effects. There is quite a lot to be said for attempting to divert demand from the West Midlands to Scotland; but when the actual upshot is that jobs are created in Scotland at the expense of the North West and then one has to adopt separate measures to protect such intermediate areas, the logic of the policy is no longer so simple and clear cut.

Taxes to Influence the Balance of Payments

A third example of selective intervention is in the balance of payments area. The well-known Brookings Report on the UK economy[7] advocated a policy of taxing import-intensive and subsidizing export-intensive industries. The logic of this is clear enough: there are grounds for arguing that the UK growth rate has been held back by balance of payments constraints but international agreements severely limit the scope for outright taxes on imports or subsidies on exports. Therefore there is something to be said for a process of operating on export-intensive and import-intensive industries, even though this is a *pis aller*. Again, one can accept the argument in principle but have some reservations about its practical limitations. Heavier taxes on import-intensive industries would seem to mean extra taxes on food, drink and tobacco – none of them very promising lines for the tax gatherer; subsidies to export-intensive industries would favour such industries as cars and pottery, but then one might legitimately ask whether this might not result in heavier consumption at home rather than more sales abroad.

So our general conclusion in this section must be that selective intervention is a game to play with more than an ordinary degree of caution; just as it is the votes on the day rather than straw polls which count in general elections, so it is the overall effects

7. R. E. Caves (ed.), *Britain's Economic Prospects*, Allen & Unwin, 1968; Chap. 2, 'Fiscal Policy', by R. A. and P. B. Musgrave.

of such policies in practice rather than the partial results foreseen by tax designers which must count in the end.

Demand Management and Growth

Our last topic is the role of demand management in growth promotion. There are two main areas of controversy about the way in which demand management can help the growth rate. The first is the optimal level of employment or output. On the one hand, a level of actual output close to that of potential output may produce various bottlenecks and inefficiencies in the economy. On the other, it can be maintained that with a given growth rate a higher level of initial output will give larger annual increments of output and that, in addition, there will be a greater all-round confidence, willingness to invest, etc. Moreover, the larger the cumulative output over a given period of time, the more opportunity for 'learning by doing'. The second area of controversy is the optimum degree of *fluctuations* in output and employment, as distinct from optimum *levels*. It is tempting here to jump to the conclusion that the less the amplitude of such fluctuations, the better for growth. But those who do so must be reminded of the post-war economic history of Japan – a remarkably high growth rate but also very pronounced fluctuations. Of course, it can be argued that the Japanese growth rate might have been even higher if it had not been for these fluctuations, but that assertion would take a very great deal of swallowing.

Finally, even if we were clear about precisely how demand management impinges on the growth rate, how easy is it in fact to manage demand by changing tax rates? An extensive investigation into this and related subjects has recently been made by Bent Hansen[8] but so far it seems to have received very little attention in this country. There are in fact three main conclusions to be drawn from his study. First, there is no single or simple relation between the pressure of demand and the growth rate: thus, over the period 1955–65, one had high unemployment

8. B. Hansen, *Fiscal Policy in Seven Countries*, OECD, Paris, 1969.

and a high growth rate in Italy, low unemployment and a high growth rate in West Germany, and low unemployment and a low growth rate in the UK. Whereas in some countries aggregate fiscal policy helped the growth rate substantially, in others it played little part. Secondly, there was evidence that fiscal policy gradually became more expansionary and so played a part in raising growth rates over this period in all the countries studied. Thirdly, there were sharp divergences in the extent to which fiscal policy helped to stabilize the economy: in the USA it was strongly stabilizing, whereas in the UK it was actually de-stabilizing, in the sense of making fluctuations worse than they would have been in the absence of attempts to mitigate them. So the moral must be that even if one is clear about the optimum degree of fluctuations of output or employment which one would like to have, it is by no means certain that one can hit the target.

The Limited Role of Tax Policy

We have not covered more than a fraction of the subject-matter of the title. One could, for instance, say a lot about tax policy and undistributed profits, tax policy and research, tax policy and free trade. But if we have said sufficient to show that in our present state of ignorance there are severe limits to what we can hope to achieve in this field, we shall have achieved our main purpose.

10

The House of Commons and Taxation

JOHN P. MACKINTOSH*

In February 1970 the Select Committee on Procedure began an investigation of the Commons' procedure in raising revenue or rather in assenting to the executive's proposals for taxation. This was clearly the second half of the work they had undertaken in the previous session on the Commons' scrutiny of public expenditure and administration.[1] The task was interrupted by the general election, but the evidence which had then been collected was published;[2] the Committee was then re-appointed in the 1970–71 session and proceeded to complete the study. Much of this article is based on the material published by the Committee.

It is hard to understand the Commons' procedure in matters of taxation without first noticing the Standing Order, now No. 82, which says 'this House will receive no petition for any sum relating to public service or proceed upon any motion for a grant ... unless recommended from the Crown.'[3] This originated in the early eighteenth century, the object being to prevent the House voting moneys to itself or its supporters, but it is totally out of date now in a House which is under the control of the executive.

Until 1965–6, however, the old rule was in force. Thus a resolution to raise money had to be a Ways and Means resolution moved in Committee of Ways and Means and it prohibited

*The author is Labour Member of Parliament for Berwick and East Lothian and has written *The British Cabinet*, among other books.

1. *First Report of the Select Committee on Procedure, Session 1968–9, Scrutiny of Public Expenditure and Administration*, No. 410, 23 July 1969.

2. *Second Special Report from the Select Committee on Procedure 1969–70*, No. 302, 27 May 1970.

3. *Standing Orders of the House of Commons*, 1969, No. 160, p. 64.

Members from moving or recommending increases or alterations in the incidence of taxation. This was altered slightly in 1965–6 when the need for a Ways and Means Committee was abolished and the resolutions could be moved on the floor of the House itself. But the effect preventing Members from suggesting increased taxes directly or by implication remained. This in itself would have so inhibited debates that a resolution was adopted to ease the position; this device allows Members to propose new clauses that would reduce rates of tax, though it is only held to apply to fairly wide categories of tax. Thus it is possible to move to reduce a band of purchase tax or to exempt a category from selective employment tax but not to relieve specific items or groups of persons.

The old rule dates from the period when the House could carry motions against the government and is now totally out of date. Its anachronistic character is evident when it is appreciated that Members can propose increased or new charges provided the money is to come from the national insurance fund, because this is not held to be taxation. It is curious that the pointlessness of this Order has not occurred to the clerks and other observers; when asked about its abolition, the Clerk-Assistant said, 'I had not anticipated the question.'[4] The only possible defence of the Standing Order is that it cuts down the number of possible amendments and thus makes it easier for the Speaker or the Chairman of the Committee to make his selection of amendments for discussion. But it is unfortunate in that it prevents Members who accept the overall economic assessment of the Chancellor of the Exchequer from arguing for a different 'mix' of taxes; they can only ask for reductions.[5]

Leaving this restriction aside and turning to the procedure for raising revenue, the principal measure used is the Finance Bill. Under SO No. 90, at the end of his budget speech the Chancellor of the Exchequer moves that under the Provisional Collection of Taxes Act, 1968, collection shall continue till the current

4. *Second Special Report, 1969–70*, pp. 81–2.
5. ibid., p. 116.

Finance Bill is passed. Then a series of Ways and Means resolutions are moved and the Finance Bill is based on them.

First there is a general debate which deals with taxation proposals and the overall budget strategy. On taxation, as the Clerks of the House put it, 'it would seem that such argument is confined to a comparatively small number of Members, who have particular interests and knowledge in this field.'[6] Next there is the second reading of the Finance Bill founded on these resolutions and this also tends to be a fairly wide-ranging debate.

Table 1[7]   Proportion of the Debates on the Budget Resolutions and on the Second Reading of the Finance Bill spent in Discussion of Taxation

	1960 %	1961 %	1967 %	1968 %
Budget resolutions				
Day 1	32	27	51	38
Day 2	46	34	21	37
Day 3	22	40	37	21
Day 4	24	38	26	44
Average of days 1–4	31	32	34	35
Finance Bill second reading	45	48	79	64

Until 1968 the Finance Bill was taken in Committee of Ways and Means in the chamber. Then a discussion ensued as to whether it should be sent upstairs to a committee, like most other Bills, the conclusion being that it should be divided, the clauses involving issues of principle being taken on the floor of the House, while the clauses dealing with matters of detail were sent to a committee. This has proved reasonably successful and acceptable to both major parties, though inevitably a slightly longer committee stage has meant a greater leniency at a report stage.

6. ibid.
7. idem.

Table 2[8]   New Clauses in Committee on Finance Bills 1962–9

	Non-government new clauses				Time spent on all new clauses (government and non-government)
1	2	3	4 Number discussed (total of those selected and those grouped with them)	5 Number not discussed (total of those out of order, not selected or not grouped)	6
Year	Number put down	Number selected*			Hours : minutes
1962	80	21	45	35	23 : 00
1963	86	17	40	46	19 : 40
1964 (April)	64	16	39	28	22 : 11
1965	60	12	16	44	13 : 15
1966	58	12	17	41	12 : 55
1967	72	9	17	55	17 : 22
1968					
† Stg Co.	81	13	0	81	0 : 0
C. w H.	67	0	0	67	0 : 0
‡ 1969	43	5	5	38	1 : 22

*The figures in column 3 show the number of clauses actually selected, i.e., excluding clauses which were grouped with them for discussion.

†In 1968, the Finance Bill was committed to a Standing Committee of 50 Members and a timetable was imposed under SO No. 43A, with the result that new clauses were not reached. The Bill was re-committed to a Committee of the whole House with the object of giving opportunities to back-bench Members who had not been members of the Standing Committee. Two and a half days were allocated to this stage under SO No. 43A but again new clauses were not reached.

‡In 1969 six clauses and one schedule were committed to a committee of the whole House, and the remainder of the Bill and new clauses to a Standing Committee of 30 Members.

8. ibid., p. 119.

There are other taxing measures such as autumn budgets, the imposition of increased national health contributions, of tolls for crossing bridges, exceptional customs duties and export rebates, but these are relatively minor. The capacity of the House of Commons to consider and influence the raising of revenue must rest on its capacity to examine, alter and improve the major annual dose of taxation as announced in the budget and embodied in the Finance Bill.

On examination, it would appear that this is the area in which the House is most effective. When the late Mr Iain Macleod wished to illustrate the power of the House, he always turned to the Finance Bill and quoted clauses where the Opposition had moved amendments and found that, though turned down by ministers in the first instance, more or less identical amendments were brought in by the Government at report stage or in the following year's Finance Bill.

The most impressive example of such second thoughts was the case of Mr Neville Chamberlain's national defence contribution. He announced this in his budget speech in 1937. It was a tax on the growth of a firm's profits in the previous 3 years. There was such an outcry in the Conservative Party and in the City that Mr Chamberlain began to talk of concessions. But the tax remained largely unchanged in the Finance Bill and pressure mounted. In the interim, Mr Chamberlain succeeded Mr Baldwin as Prime Minister and clearly wanted to commence his period in office with the backing of finance and industry. He therefore set out new proposals in a White Paper and moved new clauses for insertion into the Finance Bill. More recent examples were in 1961, when the Government gave concessions to horticulture, and in 1962, when income-tax relief for the blind was inserted at report stage. In 1964 there were 3 important changes incorporating income-tax relief for those over 65, changes in the taxation of clubs and societies engaged in mutual trading operations, and an increase in the flexibility of the regulator clause. The 1965 Finance Bill saw a number of important amendments to the capital-gains tax and the corporation tax, while in 1968 there were changes in tax relief for married men and changes in the aggregation of children's income, as well as in life policies and aggregation for estate duty. The 1969 Finance Bill had 5 new sections moved at report stage; these sections met points made in committee on tax relief for interest payments, in connection with income and corporation tax.

Table 3[9] New Clauses on Report of Finance Bills 1962–9

Year	Number put down	Number selected*	Number discussed (total of those selected and those grouped with them)	Number not discussed (total of those out of order, selected or not grouped)	Time spent on all new clauses (government and non-government) Hours : minutes	Time spent on government new clauses Hours : minutes
1	2	3	4	5	6	7
1962	36	7	15	21	7 : 29	1 : 09
1963	20	5	8	12	8 : 29	1 : 19
1964 (April)	12	5	7	5	7 : 41	1 : 53
1965	41	9	9	32	13 : 57	5 : 11
1966	28	6	7	21	4 : 44	0 : 43
1967	15	4	4	11	2 : 26	0 : 00
1968	97	10	12	85	9 : 08	0 : 40
1969	40	5	15	25	10 : 55	5 : 30

*The figures in column 3 show the number of clauses actually selected by Mr Speaker, i.e., excluding those which were grouped with them for discussion.

9. ibid.

Given this list of changes, it may be felt that the Commons has more control over, or influence on, taxation than on most other forms of legislation. The reason for this situation is interesting. Normally, negotiations are conducted with outside interests during the preparation of legislation and the anomalies or objections that are pressed can be ironed out at this stage. Because of fear of forestalling, however, the Treasury and Inland Revenue keep their tax proposals to themselves and the first the outside bodies hear of them is the announcement on budget day. Thus the committee stage of the Finance Bill is also the negotiation stage for outside interests. It makes sense for these bodies to brief the opposition or individual back-benchers at the same time as they are pressing the government, and thus the amendments that, in the case of non-financial legislation, usually precede publication, are made through the parliamentary machine in committee or at the report stage.[10]

If this is the case, it would appear that within the present limits of influence open to the House of Commons, its effect is greater in the field of taxation than in most other areas. Yet there has been some discontent. Interestingly enough, this has come most openly and explicitly from former Treasury ministers. Mr Niall MacDermott, who was Financial Secretary to the Treasury from October 1964 to August 1967, said, 'I have always believed that a select committee ... considering taxation proposals could have several advantages for a Chancellor of the Exchequer.' The advantages, according to Mr MacDermott, would be public discussion of a proposal before the government was committed, the education of the public about sensible but unpopular taxes, and the exposure of popular but unworkable proposals. He also thought that a select committee could inform the House about possible alternative taxes and could prepare reforms for which the Treasury did not have sufficient time.[11]

Mr Selwyn Lloyd, otherwise a most cautious Conservative, came forward to say that 'a select committee ... could be of considerable help to the Chancellor of the Exchequer of the day

10. ibid., p. 84.
11. ibid., pp. 11-12.

in examining particular proposals'. He cited the deduction of interest against income, the slicing provision in estate duties, the idea of a single personal tax in place of surtax and income tax, double taxation relief, provincial variations in taxation, and depreciation allowances instead of grants for industries in development areas, as suitable subjects for such a committee. Mr Lloyd's point was that he felt the Treasury and Inland Revenue were too busy to do adequate work on these topics and that outside interests felt that they did not have a proper chance to put their points of view. Both these weaknesses could be remedied if the House of Commons had proper machinery of its own to permit full consideration of proposals for new taxes and the improvement of existing taxes.

But it would be wrong to imagine that the only critics of the situation were ex-Treasury ministers. In practice, most backbenchers tend to receive taxation proposals as something decided by the government of the day and about which they can do little. They have tended to regard the merits of different taxes as something highly complex and largely outside the limits of their knowledge. Service on the Finance Committee is seen as a task for the few financial experts in the House and as a drudge for other Members. Yet few issues have aroused more feeling in recent years than the imposition of the selective employment tax. The contrast between popular feeling and MPs' opportunities for examining claims made about the tax – its incidence, its limits, its effect on the flow of labour between manufacturing and service industries – showed how ill-equipped the House is to scrutinize existing or future taxes.

At the same time, it became evident that entry to the Common Market would certainly involve Britain in the adoption of a value-added tax; but once again the House was not in a position to start an examination of such a tax or to inform itself or the public of its implications. Yet the desire for the facts was so strong in each case that the Government had to act. In 1967 the Department of Applied Economics at Cambridge under Professor Reddaway was asked by the Treasury to report on the selective employment tax, while the National Economic Development Office commissioned a report on the value-added tax (published by HMSO in 1969).

Inevitably, the question arose whether the House of Commons could have undertaken some of this work, on the grounds that it could act as soon as Members became interested in a tax, rather than wait for the government to accede to public pressure. Also the work would help to create a body of well-informed if not expert MPs, to supplement the few who had been briefed by outside interests or had special knowledge obtained through previous training. While MPs might not have the same amount of time or expertise available as Professor Reddaway or NEDO staff, they could find out what departments had done, collect the material and combine it with outside sources of information and they could push departments into carrying out further work if the existing information was inadequate.

In fact, the obvious remedy to both the ex-ministers' complaints and the lack of information and expertise on the floor of the House was the creation of a select committee to investigate problems on the revenue side. To set up such a committee would not be an innovation in parliamentary procedure though there is no exact earlier precedent. The first select committee on taxation was appointed in 1906 by Mr Asquith after there had been prolonged public discussion about the need for an element of graduation in the, until then, flat-rate income tax. Under the chairmanship of Sir Charles Dilke, a very strong committee heard a list of impressive witnesses, 3 draft reports were submitted, and there were 22 divisions before a final report was made in favour of a distinction between 'earned' and 'unearned' income and of a graduated scale of taxation. These proposals were incorporated in the Finance Acts of 1907 and 1909–10.

Between 1906 and 1936 six other select committees were asked to examine taxation questions: one considered a possible luxury duty in 1918; another examined the duties imposed on land values by the 1909–10 Finance Act in 1919; a committee in 1920 considered the possibility of taxing the increase in wealth due to the war; a betting duty was examined in 1923; and finally, in 1936 a committee was established to report on the excise duties charged under various medical stamp acts. In each case, these committees were set up because the tax concerned was particularly complex or controversial and the Chancellor of the Exchequer wanted to have a detailed or controversial examination of the proposal without being in any way committed to it. The most interesting example was the committee on the increase in wealth because of the war and the possible methods of taxing this wealth. Austen Chamberlain at the Exchequer rejected a capital levy but wanted some levy on war wealth. He told the committee that he felt either to do nothing or to start such a tax would be unacceptable unless the public had heard the full case for and against it. So he instructed the Inland Revenue to treat the committee 'for all purposes of assistance and information as if they were the Chancellor of the Exchequer'. A great deal of evidence was heard and the Inland Revenue's proposals for a levy were eventually accepted, but were then turned down by the Government. The select committee on a betting levy set up in 1923 had its views accepted and enacted in 1926 and the committee on medicine stamp duties had its proposals (for repeal) carried in the following year.

Since the war, this kind of select committee inquiring into specific taxes has not been appointed. Estimates and public accounts committees have touched on taxation problems, but only obliquely, usually conducting their investigations to see if the tax was economically and efficiently administered. This was done in the Estimates' Committee Third Report of 1945–6 on Pay As You Earn, and in the Estimates' Committee Fourth Report of 1956–7 on aspects of customs and excise collection.[12] When the Seventh Report of 1960–61 considered Schedule A taxation, the committee (quite properly) said its terms of reference did not permit it to comment on the ethics of the tax or on alternatives, but they were allowed to express their alarm over the cost of collection.[13] A large number of detailed suggestions were made by this committee for improving the efficiency of the Inland Revenue. This office was examined again in 1968–69 when the

12. House of Commons 1945–6, No. 171, and H. of C. 1956–7, No. 128.
13. House of Commons 1960–61, No. 245.

committee concentrated on the shortage of fully-trained inspectors, the programme for putting work in computers and the internal structure of the department.[14]

The Public Accounts Committee has, likewise, from time to time pointed to loopholes which lead to loss of revenue and to anomalies and false claims, while some of the specialist committees appointed after 1966 also had a side-glance at certain aspects of taxation – the Scottish Affairs Committee, for example, examining tax rebate as opposed to investment grants as a method of attracting industry to development areas.

It is clear that these post-1945 committees have simply been looking at efficiency and value for money and have been quite unlike the select committees of the 1920s, which were considering the merits of a tax, airing a whole new problem to let the government see how the public reacted; indeed, they were operating just as Mr Selwyn Lloyd and Mr Niall MacDermott had advocated. At the same time, the need of various governments to have such work done did not diminish, except that as in so many other instances there was a tendency to turn away from Parliament to Royal Commissions, departmental committees and specially appointed outside groups to do the work. Since the war there have been the Report of the Departmental Committee on Taxation and Overseas Minerals in 1948–9;[15] the report of the Committee on the Taxation of Trading Profits in 1950–51;[16] a Committee on Purchase Tax/Utility in 1951–2;[17] a Committee on Tax-paid Stocks in 1952–3[18] and one on Purchase Tax (Valuation) in the same year;[19] a Royal Commission on the Taxation of Profits and Income;[20] a Committee on the Taxation Treatment of Provisions for Retirement in 1953;[21] a Com-

14. House of Commons 1968–9, No. 474.

15. Cmnd. 7728.

16. Cmnd. 8189.

17. Cmnd. 8452.

18. Cmnd. 8784.

19. Cmnd. 8830.

20. Its reports were, First Report, 1952–3, Cmnd. 8761; Second Report, 1953–64, Cmnd. 9105; Final Report, 1955–6, Cmnd. 9474.

21. Cmnd. 9063.

mittee on Turnover Taxation in 1963–4,[22] and the reports already mentioned on the selective employment tax and value-added tax.

So it is clear that there is a field here which the House of Commons has abandoned. This retreat has weakened its capacity to scrutinize taxation, prevented it helping ministers to consider alternatives, and reduced the relevance of Members' contributions on these matters, both on the floor of the House and in committee. In its hearing in 1969–70, the Select Committee on Procedure had two alternative solutions put before it. One was for a standing select committee on taxation which would do the kind of work undertaken by the select committees of the 1920s. But instead of being instructed to examine a particular tax and to report, the committee would be left free to take up an existing tax, to examine present anomalies, to consider future departures in taxation or to relate taxation to other aspects of social and fiscal policy, as the committee felt inclined. Such a committee would require a staff and would have the power to summon ministers, as well as any official or outside evidence.

The alternative put forward by Mr J. H. Robertson and by Messrs Samuel Brittan and Peter Jay (who gave joint evidence) was for a select committee on economic affairs (SCEA). This was a more ambitious proposal based on the analogy of the Joint Economic Committee of the United States Congress. Such a body would work on current economic assessments; it would consider the long-term implications of financing the levels of public expenditure set out in the annual White Papers, and it would also investigate special problems such as the alleviation of poverty, international monetary reform, and trading policy.

Such a committee would require a full-time staff of experts (a staff of 5 economists was suggested) working under the direction of the committee of MPs, and it would produce a stream of reports designed to give MPs briefs and to raise the whole quality of debate inside and outside the House. The committee would both undertake and commission research and operate through up to half a dozen sub-committees pursuing simultaneous inquiries.

22. Cmnd. 2300.

In the eyes of its protagonists, the SCEA would do the background work for the scrutiny of both expenditure and taxation. Indeed, the two sides of the approach to public finance should not be separated, Brittan and Jay quoting the Plowden Committee's remarks that 'it should be possible to form worthwhile judgements about whether a certain prospective size and pattern of public expenditure is likely to stimulate or to retard the growth of Gross National Product, and is likely to outrun the resources available to finance it'.[23] Clearly such a committee would be able to provide Parliament with the kind of 'counter Civil Service' which many legislatures have found they need if they are to compete with the growing expertise of government and the sheer complexity of the issues coming before them.

The objections to both a standing select committee on taxation and the broader select committee on economic affairs came principally from the Treasury. While it was prepared to disclose its annual rearrangement of the five-year rolling programme on public expenditure to Parliament, the Treasury appeared to think that the revenue side of the account was quite different. Yet both are clearly interdependent in the eyes of the Plowden Committee and in those of most economists.[24] The Treasury spokesman, Sir Douglas Allen, seemed convinced that any such committee would be asking Civil Servants to exhibit their value judgement, their opinions on policy. He also thought that any form of evidence – whether forthcoming with facts or reticent – would give observers clues as to the department's thinking and that this would lead to anticipation of government decisions and even to the forestalling of financial operations.[25]

It is hard to convince those with such fears that examinations can be conducted and possibilities elucidated without in any way reducing the options open to the government in the short run. And as to forestalling, governments have themselves discounted this by using the device of a Green Paper (over the regional

23. *Select Committee on Procedure 1969–70*, No. 302, p. 152.

24. See the evidence on this submitted by Professors Wiseman and Peacock, ibid., pp. 93–111.

25. *Select Committee on Procedure 1968–9*, No. 40, pp. 227–36.

employment premium) and by putting specific problems to Royal Commissions and departmental committees. Detailed new tax proposals are debated for months in the US Congress without any such problem arising.

The general election of June 1970 prevented the Select Committee on Procedure reporting on the work it had done or on the evidence it had collected in the 1969–70 session. When Parliament reassembled, the committee was reconstituted and heard further evidence from the new Conservative Government (in the shape of Mr Maurice Macmillan, then Chief Secretary to the Treasury, and Mr William Whitelaw, then Lord President of the Council and Leader of the House) before reporting. The Treasury also put in a further memorandum.[26]

In this evidence, both written and oral, ministers and officials emphatically maintained the previous stand of the Treasury. The memorandum said 'we share the view that it is of the utmost importance that Parliament should have a more effective role than at present in the control of fiscal and economic policy – as a matter of democratic principle',[27] but would accept no proposal for a standing committee of any kind to scrutinize either taxation proposals or the wider aspects of economic policy. The objections raised no new points, concentrating on the alleged constitutional difficulties of committee work, derogation from the floor of the House, overwork of MPs, the awkwardness confronting officials in discussing the details of taxation and of economic policy, and the extra burden such activity would place on their time.

The Select Committee, in its Report, largely rejected these arguments. In the interim period, the Conservative Government had announced in a Green Paper, *Select Committees of the House of Commons*,[28] its intention to accept the Select Committee on Procedure's recommendation and set up a Select Committee on Expenditure, though this body was to be somewhat smaller

26. See *First Report from the Select Committee on Procedure 1970–71, Scrutiny of Taxation*, No. 276, February 1971.

27. ibid., p. 2.

28. Cmnd. 4507, October 1970. See also the debate on the Green Paper in Hansard, Vol. 806, No. 33, for 12 November 1970.

and consist of 45 Members. But it would have powers to divide
into sub-committees, each of which was to scrutinize a special
field of public expenditure with a general or coordinating
committee, which would examine the statistics, comment on the
information available to the sub-committees and prepare the
report of the committee. Taking advantage of this step forward,
the Select Committee on Procedure recommended 'that sufficient
Members should be added to the Expenditure Committee to form
a Sub-Committee on Taxation and Finance of that committee',
that the whole committee be renamed 'the Expenditure and
Finance Committee', and that its terms of refence be extended.
Looking ahead, the Report foresaw

that the Sub-Committee may, in the course of its inquiries into the
economic implications of taxation, and in response to a growing
demand in the House, be led to examine wider economic issues. Such
inquiries would enable the Sub-Committee to build up, for themselves
and for the House, a more balanced and comprehensive picture of the
economic background to taxation and the financing of public expenditure. If the work of the Sub-Committee were to develop along
these lines, Your Committee consider that a strong argument might
then exist for the development of the Sub-Committee into an independent Select Committee on Taxation and Economic Affairs.[29]

There was no indication that the Government would accede to
this request and when the annual White Paper on Public Expenditure was published in early 1971, it revealed its sensitivity
about the amount of information available to the House of
Commons by refusing to publish either the medium-term economic assessment (compiled by the Treasury and used in pre-
paring the public expenditure forecast) or estimated receipts
from taxation. But when the Chancellor of the Exchequer presented his Financial Statement and Budget Report in March
1971, he went some of the way with the demands for more information on taxation by presenting Green Papers on *Value-added
Tax*[30] and on *Reform of the Corporation Tax*.[31]

29. *First Report from the Select Committee on Procedure 1970–71, Scrutiny
of Taxation*, pp. xxi–xxii.
30. Cmnd. 4621.
31. Cmnd. 4630.

As a result, several speakers pressed the Treasury spokesmen during the budget debate. The Chairman of the Select Committee on Procedure, Mr Robin Turton, asked 'if the Chancellor is able to deal with the problems of taxation three years ahead, why cannot Parliament do the same? Why cannot committees of the House look forward into these projections? ... Surely the object of Green Papers should be consultation with Parliament.'[32] Sir Brandon Rhys Williams, Mr David Ginsburg and Mr David Marquand also pressed the point, the latter saying:

In my view it would be intolerable if the government were to consult a whole range of outside interests on the proposals in the two Green Papers and were never to submit them to detailed scrutiny by a select committee. It is not possible in exchanges across the floor, or even at the committee stage of a Bill upstairs, to scrutinize such proposals with the sort of detail and seriousness which they require.[33]

In reply, Mr Maurice Macmillan repeated the Treasury arguments against any select committee examination of these Green Papers and added that as the Government intended to introduce a value-added tax in April 1973, there was no time for a select committee to meet, consider the question and report. This generally negative reaction was not really mitigated by the saving clause that 'what I say now is not necessarily a final view.'[34] However he was prepared to consider a select committee on the corporation tax and this was, in fact, appointed five weeks later. If Parliament is to recover some of its former capacity to understand taxation, to explain the issues to the public, to put ideas to the government and to stimulate public reaction, there will have to be a new attitude to this matter on the part of the Treasury and its ministers. The one encouraging feature of the 1970–71 debates was the statement by the Leader of the House, Mr William Whitelaw, that he had no intention, in his period of office, of presiding over a continual decline in the influence of the House of Commons.[35]

32. Hansard, Vol. 814, No. 116, col. 1584, 31 March 1971.
33. ibid., No. 117, col. 1793, 1 April 1971.
34. ibid., No. 119, col. 49, 5 April 1971.
35. ibid., cols. 871–3, 3 November 1970.

II

The Long-term Planning of Taxation

SIR RICHARD CLARKE*

In the last ten years under both Conservative and Labour governments there has been considerable progress in the long-term planning and control of public expenditure. This was begun by the Plowden Report on the Control of Public Expenditure of July 1961, and there has since been a continuous stream of White Papers expounding the new procedures and publishing the governments' forward estimates of expenditure.[1] There is now a regular procedure for publishing these projections; and every government must face the responsibility and discipline of publishing them. A select committee procedure has been set up to examine these projections, to report upon them, and to enable Parliament to discuss them meaningfully.

Public Expenditure and Resources

The original driving idea was to relate the prospective growth of public expenditure to the economic resources which are likely to be available when the expenditure is incurred. Most expenditure takes time to mature. New spending programmes in defence or education or roads take a long time to come to fruition after the original decisions have been taken to embark upon them. The decision to undertake them must therefore depend not upon the situation at the moment but upon the situation in two or three

*The author was Permanent Secretary of the Ministry of Technology from 1966–70, and prior to that a Second Permanent Secretary of the Treasury.

1. See Sir Samuel Goldman's lecture on 'The Presentation of Public Expenditure Proposals to Parliament' in the autumn 1970 issue of *Public Administration*.

years' time; and it must therefore be based upon a view of what the economy or the tax-payer will be able to afford in two or three years' time, and even farther ahead. It was the lack of an apparatus for making these appraisals of the huge spending programmes of the late 1950s that led to the Plowden 'approach'. The purpose, in short, was to get better immediate public expenditure decisions.

The subsequent practice was to relate the prospective total public expenditure[2] to the future economic resources (Gross National Product and its constituents) and not to receipts from taxation. The subject was conceived in terms of Gross National Product (GNP) and so-called physical resources – in 'real terms' rather than in 'money terms'. The big programmes for which improved decision-making was needed were expenditures on goods and services, both current and investment, together with the social security benefits which are virtually all immediately spent on goods and services by the pensioners and other state beneficiaries and thus could reasonably be so regarded. By the late 1950s, projections of GNP and its main constituents were being regularly prepared in the Treasury in terms of a concept of 'constant prices', and so this all fitted together naturally. Taxation on the other hand is essentially a 'money' concept and not a 'real terms' concept. The idea of 'public sector receipts at constant prices' is an elusive one, both in respect of taxes on expenditure and also in respect of taxes on income and capital. So from the start the expenditure projections were considered in relation to the GNP projections in terms of 'constant prices' or perhaps more precisely 'constant value of money'.

One way to do this is to relate the prospective growth of public expenditure to the prospective growth of GNP, arguing that the rate of growth of the former should not exceed the rate of growth that could be reasonably expected in the latter. But this approach has led nowhere in the past. There was nothing obviously sacrosanct about the current proportion of public expenditure to GNP in any particular year: many people in all political parties

2. There are of course problems of definition, as Mr Samuel Brittan says in his article, but they are not material to my argument.

have favoured the allocation of a larger share of GNP to public expenditure; and so the bare ratio carried no conviction. In the glad confident morning of 'indicative planning' in the early 1960s, moreover, it was always possible to make a prospective growth of public expenditure look tolerable by assuming that there was going to be an increase in the rate of growth of GNP; and it was not until the bitter experience of the middle and late 1960s had been digested that a more cautious and realistic projection of growth rates for the national economy came to be acceptable to public opinion.

Public Spending versus Private Consumption

For development of a rational argument, therefore, the GNP must be broken down into its constituent parts. Public expenditure is thus shown as being in competition with the balance of payments, private investment and private consumption. This kind of projection must be made internally consistent; so the implications of assuming an excessive growth rate or a high public expenditure ratio have to be brought out into the open. This leads to an appraisal as follows, with the subsequent conclusion: if present public expenditure programmes are carried out (assuming constant prices); if we can reasonably expect GNP to increase at x per cent per annum; if we succeed in achieving our target surplus in the balance of payments; if private investment rises at p per cent per annum, *then* private consumption will be able to rise in the next few years by no more than q per cent per annum.

The problem which ministers would then have to face is that of weighing the public reaction to the achievement of the public expenditure plans against the public reaction to a restriction of the growth of private consumption to q per cent per annum, including in this, of course, the whole variety of middle positions. This procedure may be presented as a triumph of logic and lucidity; but in practice it too risks getting nowhere. Very few people are capable of visualizing the difference in terms of public satisfaction and public welfare between an increase in private consumption of say 2 per cent per annum for years and one of 2½ per cent per annum. But the difference in 4 years' time is £600 million a year, and this is the difference between doing a great many of the 'marginal' things that governments want to do in public expenditure and being able to do none of them.

In 24 post-war years to 1970, the average annual increase of consumers' expenditure (in real terms) has been a little below 2½ per cent. In 6 of these 24 years, the increase was 4 per cent or more. In 5, it was an increase of less than 1 per cent or a decrease. In 8 of the 24 years, the increase was between 2 per cent and 2¾ per cent: how many people could identify even in retrospect these 'near-average' years, let alone distinguish between the situation of the consumer public at the upper and the lower ends of this 'near-average' range?[3] The ministers who make the decisions and the senior officials who advise them cannot reasonably be expected to have the conceptual grasp and imagination to consider their decisions and argue them in these terms. One can of course easily distinguish between the 'never had it so good' consumer boom of 4 per cent per annum and the 'austerity' of 1 per cent per annum, but in order to make sense of public expenditure decisions by this route one has to distinguish between 2 per cent per annum and 2½ per cent per annum, which is a different kind of thing altogether. Ministers and officials can judge between two public expenditure programmes, and say that it is better to give marginally more resources to health than to overseas aid or whatever it may be. But they cannot in practical terms weigh in the same scales these public expenditures against the comparative prospective value to the community of an estimated annual rate of growth of 2 per cent as distinct from 2½ per cent in the aggregate of private consumption.

The essence is government responsibility. The public expenditure programmes are the clear and accepted responsibility of government (including for this purpose the local authorities as

3. Increases of 4 per cent or more: 1953, 1954, 1955, 1959, 1960, 1963. Increases of less than 1 per cent (or decrease): 1948, 1951, 1952, 1956, 1969. Increases of between 2 per cent and 2¾ per cent (in ascending order): 1957, 1966, 1967, 1962, 1968, 1958, 1961, 1950.

'government'). The aggregate of private consumption and its growth and distribution are not the responsibility of government. They are affected by government's decisions to the extent that these affect incomes, prices, taxes and saving decisions: but they are determined by the decisions of millions of people in the background of events and circumstances which are not determined by government and are indeed only indirectly affected by government. It is not easy to get a clear concept of the aggregate of public expenditure and what it means in terms of public satisfaction and welfare, even though government is responsible for every bit of it in detail. But to get a similar concept of the implications for the national well-being of future changes in the aggregate of private consumption, which is completely outside the detailed control and responsibility of government, is not possible. In any government or Parliament, or in the columns of the newspapers, the generalized claims of private consumption (for which the government does not have specific responsibility) will tend to rank second to the specific claims of attractive proposals for spending public money. A specific proposal, backed by an important public opinion lobby and within the field of government responsibility, is always easier to expound and defend than a consideration of the general well-being of the whole community.

The Significance of Taxation

The confrontation of public expenditure programmes with first, the prospective growth of GNP, and then the prospective availability of resources for the growth of personal consumption, is thus unlikely to provide a practical basis for government decision-making, because we are not comparing like with like in government responsibility. If however the implications for taxes could be put on the other side of the balance from the public expenditure programmes, we should be weighing one set of government decisions against another and, in terms of political responsibility, assuredly measuring like against like. This is the strength of matching the growth of public expenditure against the growth of public sector receipts as well as against the growth and development of the national economy.[4]

Experience suggests that changes in rates of taxation and changes in consumer expenditure tend to follow each other (of course in opposite directions) over the four- or five-year periods which are relevant to public expenditure planning. Large increases in consumer expenditure are likely, over periods of years, to be associated with reductions in rates of taxation, and vice versa. So the two ways of looking at the problem may not be very different in practice. The following table illustrates this:

	Average annual increase or decrease in the rates of taxation announced in the budget as % of GNP	*Average annual increase in consumer expenditure at constant prices*
	% p.a.	% p.a.
1947–52	$\frac{1}{2}$	1.0
1953–64	$-\frac{1}{2}$	3.3
1965–70	1	2.0

But of course there are very great problems in working with taxes; that is why this is not yet systematized. One cannot say in advance what the relation should be in any future year between the aggregate of public expenditure and the aggregate of public sector receipts. Taxation decisions, unlike most public expenditure decisions, make their impact on the economy quickly; and their purpose nowadays is just as much as an instrument in the short-term demand management of the national economy as the source of revenue to pay for public expenditure. The public expenditure decisions must be taken two or three years ahead; what should one therefore assume about the state of the economy at that point in time, about the size of the budget surplus required, and about whether a restrictive or an expansive fiscal policy will then be needed?

Again, the receipts from taxation are particularly difficult to predict, for, unlike the relevant public expenditures, they cannot be expressed in terms of 'constant prices'. As money incomes rise,

4. Sir Richard Clarke, 'The Management of the Public Sector of the National Economy', Stamp Memorial Lecture, 1964, Athlone Press.

people move into higher tax brackets and pay proportionately more tax; so that the total tax receipts are disproportionately altered by inflation – and one cannot make a happy 'adjustment for inflation' by deflating with a price index number. When one thinks in terms of taxes one leaves the world of 'GNP at constant prices' and 'expenditure in real terms', and moves into the world (what many might call the 'actual' world) of calculations and aggregates in money. My own belief is that this must be done, and that the conventional analysis in terms of constant prices assumes away the actual problems of public policy in an inflationary period, just as the conventional pre-Keynesian analysis in terms of full employment assumed away the actual problems of public policy in the period of mass unemployment during the 1930s. But it must be admitted that there are great practical difficulties here both of concept and of calculation.

Long-term Taxation Policy

There is also the mystique of the ministerial handling of taxation, the notion that it is the particular private preserve of the Chancellor of the Exchequer, and not a suitable subject for wide discussion within the government. This was historically designed, very prudently, to protect the secrecy of government deliberations about taxation, and so to minimize the dangers of leakage and scandals within the government; this is still right for what one might call the tactical decisions of taxation, and the fewer people who know about an impending change in a tax rate the better. When one is considering long-term tax policy in relation to long-term expenditure policy, however, the secrecy argument cannot be given any weight. The Green Papers on the structure of taxes together with the 1971 budget were a welcome step forward; and the problems of long-term tax policy should surely be debated openly with the facts on the table, just like those of defence or education. In my opinion, all governments should have just the same duty to publish their long-term taxation policy as they now have to publish their expenditure policy.

Indeed, this obligation to publish taxation policy is really essential for the control of public expenditure. In order to get realistic expenditure decisions governments must argue them, both within themselves and outside, against their taxation implications. Only so can the straight government responsibilities for expenditure be matched against other equally specific government responsibilities instead of against misty macro-economic figures about consumption, investment, etc. I do not assert that the government should publish a table of future revenue in strict parallel with the forward estimation of public expenditure. This would be meaningless unless it were founded upon a specific forecast about the future rate of inflation, because of the disproportionate sensitivity of tax receipts to inflation to which I referred earlier; and governments will always be reluctant to publish such a forecast, partly for the obvious political reasons, but even more because of the effect that such announcements would be likely to have upon the actual course of events. Some forecasts by governments set up forces in the economy which are self-fulfilling.

This difficulty could be mitigated if the government were to announce an anti-inflation objective for 4 or 5 years ahead – i.e. a price objective to the securing of which all their policies would be committed. The projections of resources, expenditure and revenue could then all be based on this objective – not a forecast but an intention. Failing a completely new departure of this kind, the conceptual and practical difficulties are very great; although even without such a departure I believe it would still be possible to give some guide to the bearing of long-term expenditure upon long-term taxes. The way in which the government's taxation objectives and priorities should be fitted in with the public expenditure objectives and priorities is discussed in my series of lectures, 'New Trends in Government'.[5]

Aspects of Fiscal Policy

The government therefore needs to have and publish a long-

5. Civil Service College, HMSO, 1971.

term taxation plan, not only because taxation[6] is one of the central functions of governments, but also because this is how to bring the spending decisions of the government into proper perspective. A long-term plan for taxation must clearly take all the aspects of taxation into account, namely:

1. Short-term demand management.
2. Social policy (i.e. the use of taxation to change the distribution of income and other social objectives).
3. Economy policy (i.e. the effect of taxes on incentives for individuals and for companies, and the implications of this for economic growth and other economic objectives).
4. The efficient raising of money to pay for public spending – simplicity, cheapness of collection, acceptability and fairness between tax-payers.

The merit of requiring the government to present a long-term plan is that the government must then find a structure which gives the best mix of its objectives under all the above heads. Otherwise governments will focus upon whichever objective happens to seem most important at the moment and will ignore the others. The great tax changes earlier in this century were derived mainly from social policy. The health of the economy has had low priority since the Second World War but it was predominant in the great fiscal measures of the nineteenth century and in the adoption of tariff protection in 1932. Many of the main attributes of the British taxation system flow from (4) above, but governments usually have to sacrifice (4) to gain advantages under (1) and (2). In the last 25 years, it is probably true to say that considerations of short-term demand management have been predominant.

Short-term Demand Management

It would be desirable, if it could be done, to separate the short-term demand management aspect of taxation from the true fiscal and social and economic aspects; for the concentration on the

6. 'Taxation' here means 'public sector receipts', for it must include local rates, national insurance contributions and the surpluses, if any, of the nationalized industries.

former tends to drive out attention and effort from the latter. The core of most annual budgets nowadays is the short-term economic situation, and the questions of tax structure and their relationship to public expenditure tend to be subordinated to it. Mr Barber's 1971 budget was a very distinguished exception to this, but such exceptions have been rare. If we could split off the short-term demand management aspect of taxation and handle it separately, this would make it possible to give proper weight to basic fiscal problems and thus to the long-term place of the public sector in the economy and to the relationship between government and the productive power of the economy.

The short-term demand management aspect of taxation calls only rarely for changes in rates of taxation which are significant in relation to the size of the national economy. In the 26 years from 1946 to 1971, rates of taxation were increased in 10 budgets (where there were two budgets in a year I add them together), reduced in 10 budgets, and left virtually unchanged in the other 6 budgets. But only 8 times in the 26 have the changes been significantly more than 1 per cent of GNP – 4 of these up (1947, 1951, 1965, 1966) and 4 of them down (1953, 1959, 1963 and 1971). In more than half the years when changes were made they were quite small (less than about £200 million at present GNP); and one doubts whether the need for changes of this amplitude can be diagnosed with enough assurance to justify such use of the taxation instrument.

On those occasions, about one third of the 26 years, in which the case for action for short-term demand management is clear, the natural course is to spread the fiscal action as widely as possible over the economy, and not to concentrate it upon particular people or particular industries. I would like to see the new-style unified income tax and the value-added tax (VAT) designated as the sole taxes to be used for this purpose. A 'regulator' could no doubt be incorporated in VAT to entitle the government to raise or lower the rates at any time within certain limits. If it becomes possible through computerization to collect income tax in Pay As You Earn (PAYE) on a non-cumulative basis, this would open the way to 'regulator' action there also, at very much shorter notice than is now possible and with a wider-spread effect on the economy.

If the fiscal measures for short-period demand management could be concentrated on two taxes with a 'regulator' provision for each, not used often – perhaps once in two or three years – this would be a more effective demand-management instrument; and the budget procedure would be freed from the present excessive concentration on the short period. This would fit in well with the concept of a long-term policy for taxation side by side with a long-term policy for public expenditure – with the emphasis on the impact of both taxation and public expenditure on social policy on the one hand, and on the incentives for economic efficiency and growth on the other. This would have the added merit of getting away from the circus atmosphere of the present budget format, the exaggerated ritual of taking the nation's temperature, and the publicized hopes and fears of whether the Chancellor of the Exchequer is going to 'take something away' or 'give us something back' on 'his day'. This would begin to get the discussion of taxation and public expenditure policy, which is the most important responsibility and field of action of the government (and not of the Chancellor of the Exchequer alone) on the economic front, onto a proper long-term basis with its time unit being the rolling life of a Parliament. Indeed, it is only by concentrating upon long-term policy in the fields in which the government can actually take action, instead of on short-term expedients and exhortation, that it will become possible to develop an effective campaign against inflation.

Long-term Taxation Structure

The purpose of this chapter is to advocate a long-term taxation policy and the setting up of institutional arrangements that will help governments to create it, publish it, and arrange for effective public discussion of it. I think this is more important at the present stage than detailed argument about how the structure should be reformed, especially as Mr Barber's 1971 budget has set in motion a formidable series of reforms which must clearly provide the starting point for all further discussion. Taking social and economic considerations together, however, I do not think there is very much doubt about what needs to be put right. I have found much to agree with in Professor Cedric Sandford's new book,[7] which was prepared a long time before the 1971 budget but which has anticipated it in a number of important respects.

It has been common ground for generations that the tax system should be progressive, but it is only comparatively recently that it has been possible to calculate together the incidence of all taxes, direct and indirect, including local rates and national insurance contributions, on people at each income level. The conclusion which Professor Sandford reaches, and which in his opinion does not conflict seriously with the data as they now exist, is that it is only in the upper 2 per cent range of household incomes (where the surtax begins to bite) that our tax system is progressive at all: below that, very broadly speaking, taxation is proportionate to income. The lower-income groups get more social security benefits, so the total effect of the intervention of the state is progressive; but it is the structure of benefits (i.e. the government expenditure) and not the tax system (except in the surtax range) that reduces the inequality of income. There are also great anomalies in the system below the surtax level, especially when the incidence of benefits is combined with the incidence of taxation; much reform is needed to get a smooth progression giving effect to a rational and self-consistent social concept.

One important element is the treatment of families compared with single people. This should be looked at, again taking social service benefits as well as taxation into account, predominantly 'horizontally', comparing the situation of people with and without dependents at each income level. Mr Piachaud's essay shows that the minimum scales laid down by the Supplementary Benefits Commission (November 1970) imply that a married man with 2 children on the 'poverty level' needs 1.87 times as much spending power as a single man, and a married man with 4

7. Professor C. T. Sandford, *Realistic Tax Reform*, Chatto & Windus and Charles Knight, 1971.

children needs 2.37 times as much. A single man or woman with £20 a week would then (after taxes and rates and national insurance contributions as they then were) be on a standard of living about 50 per cent above that of the married man with 2 children (and 75 per cent above the one with 4 children) on the same earning level. Suppose that at higher income levels the same relationship holds between the 'needs' of single people and people with dependents – which appears to be a modest assessment of the cost of dependents, or a generous estimate of the economies of scale in household expenditure. A single man or woman with £3,000 a year would then have a standard of living about 75 per cent above that of a married man with 2 children with the same income, and well over double that of the married man with 4 children. At every income level in our society, the difference between the standard of living of those with and without dependents is very striking, and is at least as great at the middle-class income levels as at the lower.[8] A substantial differential is an integral part of the family system. But how large should it be? Certainly the 'vertical' comparison which is often made, between the tax reliefs for children and other dependents of the relatively well-to-do and the family allowances available for the people who are too poor to get tax reliefs, misses the point altogether. The true comparison must be the 'horizontal' one between people at the same income level.

The Top 2 Per Cent

At the top 2 per cent of household incomes, where the progression of taxation is uniquely steep in the advanced world, this country constitutes the worst of all possibilities. Such penal rates of taxation are levied on incomes and on estates that huge incentives are created for people so to manage their affairs that they avoid paying them; many of the ablest people in the country are

8. In the Civil Service, the standard of living of a Permanent Secretary, married with 2 dependent children, would on the same analysis be no higher than that of a single man or woman Assistant Secretary three levels below, which is the regular career grade of the Service.

employed in advising their employers and clients how to do this. For the professional and entrepreneurial classes, the tax system undoubtedly creates disincentives to increased work and to risk-taking, to the great damage of the economy. It may well be that the impact of this taxation system, which throughout the last 25 years has penetrated to the roots of the personal and collective behaviour of the relatively well-to-do, has been one of the major forces which have created the deficiencies of management and absence of enterprise characteristic of the national situation; and the habits of the upper reaches of society tend to spread throughout the whole. So great has the pressure been on people to arrange their affairs so as to avoid tax – an entirely legitimate preoccupation, quite distinct from illegal action to evade tax – that the truth could well be that less revenue has been collected by the state from the top 2 per cent of household incomes, both from income and from capital taxes, than could have been obtained if the progression had been less violent and the system more widely-based and acceptable. The organization of tax avoidance has become so deep-rooted in the national economy and is backed by such huge resources of accountants and tax lawyers that a tremendous change would be needed in order to remove this distortion from the economic system and create economically constructive pressures throughout the fiscal system.

Professor Sandford thinks that this change can be made only by looking at taxes on income and capital on the top 2 per cent together. He believes that it would be possible to get the same revenue from the well-to-do in a manner which did much less damage to economic incentives and gave much less encouragement to tax avoidance by greatly reducing the marginal taxation on the higher incomes (he proposes a maximum of 55 per cent tax on the marginal slice of incomes of £10,000 a year or more), and completely reshaping the taxes on capital. However this may be, this issue is crucial to the reconstruction of the national economy and indeed to the future of the revenue. Mr Barber's 1971 budget made a start in the right direction, but it cannot be seriously regarded as more than a first step. The capital taxes require much more thought; and the future of the corporation taxes is bound to follow the development in Europe, for the common fiscal treatment of industry throughout Europe will become necessary in the interests of our own industry.

Indirect Taxes

The problems of indirect taxation will increasingly become subsumed in the working of the value-added tax, when it is enacted. VAT is an expensive tax to collect; and its main attraction is in its conformity with Europe. However, it has some advantages compared with our present system because it will cover a wider range of consumer goods and services with one system of tax. This is good for short-term demand management; and it would also stop the differentially high taxation of the motorcar and other mass-production industries, whose international competitive power is weakened by the restriction of the home market through specially high purchase tax. Some of these advantages could be obtained without VAT, by replacing purchase tax and selective employment tax (SET) with a general sales tax on consumer goods and services; but it is unlikely that any government would do this except under pressure from outside, through having to conform to a common European pattern. When we have VAT, however, there will still be a number of matters to be cleared up in the indirect taxation field, notably the classical revenue duties. At some stage it will be necessary to see how local rates and national insurance contributions fit into the total taxation system.

Declaring a Long-term Policy

There is no obvious reason why governments should not announce their intentions about tax structure several years in advance; this was a marked characteristic of Mr Gladstone's budgets: it is a most welcome feature of Mr Barber's 1971 budget speech. To my mind a failure to do this is evidence of a government's lack of direction and constructive power. Of course, if so much is loaded onto a Chancellor of the Exchequer that he has little time for formulating a taxation policy, or if the country has 13 Chancellors in 27 years,[9] one cannot expect to have a long-term policy for taxation or anything else in economic affairs. If, however, a government can evolve and announce a long-term policy on taxation structure and then be seen to be implementing it year by year, this demonstration of sustained purpose can hardly fail to have electoral advantages.

This procedure allows the maximum scope for public and parliamentary discussion of the details of the structure, and thus the greatest expectation that the legislation will prove itself efficient. It is in this area, rather than in the one concerning the concepts and principles of the tax structure, or the actual numbers of the rates at which taxes are levied, that Green Papers, parliamentary select committees, and consultations between the revenue departments and the professional bodies concerned have the biggest contribution to make.

The aggregate of tax receipts, which is the second element in a long-term taxation policy, is implicit in the publication of a long-term expenditure policy, provided that one can adequately enable the forward statements about tax intentions to exclude the use of the taxes as 'regulators' for short-period demand management. This is done without difficulty on the expenditure side: nobody expects the estimates of the cost of unemployment benefit to be on any other basis but a formally assumed level of unemployment. It is more difficult on the taxation side, but it is clearly not impossible provided that sensible conventions are established.

In my opinion, every government should make a long-term statement about its objective for the aggregate of tax receipts. The choice between higher and lower public expenditure and taxes is an essential one, both in political philosophy and in governmental practice; no government should be allowed to evade it. Indeed, the difference in timing between public expenditure

9. From the end of 1944 to the end of 1971: Sir John Anderson, Dr Dalton, Sir Stafford Cripps, Mr Gaitskell, Mr Butler, Mr Macmillan, Mr Thorneycroft, Mr Heathcoat-Amory, Mr Selwyn Lloyd, Mr Maudling, Mr Callaghan, Mr Jenkins, (Mr Macleod, not included in the 13), Mr Barber.

decisions and the consequent taxation implications makes it particularly important that the government should be seen to be handling both at the same time.

From the start of any government's life there is an implicit choice: whether the tax objectives or the expenditure objectives are overriding. If the former, this must be reflected in the earliest expenditure decisions; in any government the pressures for higher public expenditure, both from within and from outside, are so strong and continuous that they can be effectively resisted only by confrontation with tax objectives. The normal forces of inertia, especially when the taxes are regarded as being the personal prerogative of the Chancellor of the Exchequer and not a matter of collective responsibility of the Cabinet for policy formation, will always tend to favour the expenditure objectives. It is clear in retrospect that the successive governments from the mid-1950s to 1970 really regarded their expenditure objectives as ranking first, with taxation as the residual: from 1957–8 onwards, the symbolic moment being the resignation of all the Treasury ministers in January 1958, the proportion of government expenditure to Gross National Product steadily increased. Mr Heath's Government started in the opposite direction. Time will show whether they can sustain a continuing impact on rates of taxation; but I feel that no government can do this without nailing their colours firmly and publicly to the mast.

The third possible element in a long-term taxation plan is to nominate objectives for particular rates of taxation, e.g. to reduce the new 30 per cent for the reconstructed tax on earned income to 25 per cent in the lifetime of a Parliament, and to limit the new VAT to 10 per cent (or whatever a suitable figure may be). Even if these are government objectives only in the same sense as the health, education or defence programmes, they are of great importance to the working of the government. There could never be a convention that a government should nominate tax-rate objectives of this kind; and only a government attaching great importance to tax reduction would do so. But there is no doubt about the force that such a nomination of specific tax-rate objectives would have in informing the whole strategy of a government.

Conclusions

1. As the next stage in the development of long-term fiscal policy, every government should announce a long-term taxation policy covering both the form and structure of taxation and the aggregate of taxation (i.e. the choice between expenditure and taxes at the margin).

2. The use of tax changes for short-period demand management should be separated as far as possible from the consideration of 'normal' fiscal policy (possibly by designating certain taxes for this purpose under 'regulator' conditions).

3. Long-term taxation policy should in particular seek to bring about an effective progression (taking all taxes and social security benefits into account) in taxes on income and capital; a proper differential between those with and without dependents throughout the income structure; and the removal of economic disincentives and incentives for tax avoidance.

4. A government taking taxation seriously will do well to consider formulating and announcing specific long-term objectives for the rates of the leading taxes, both in order to sharpen discussion within the government on expenditure questions and to establish effective public understanding of the government's policy.

5. The implementation of government policy for the form and structure of taxation should be conducted as publicly as possible.

12

Social Security and Taxation

BRIAN ABEL-SMITH*

In the attempt to redistribute resources in favour of poor families, more and more mechanisms have been developed which in total substantially reduce the reward from earning more. Universal benefits give rise to heavy revenue requirements – from taxation or contributions. Selective benefits or rebates have lower revenue requirements, but make heavy demands on marginal income simply because they are selective. Despite all the mechanisms for redistributing income, the problem of poverty is still unresolved. We do not redistribute enough to 'solve' the poverty problem and much of what is on offer is not taken up.

One conclusion which could be drawn from this analysis is that future policy should concentrate on raising minimum earnings because of the limits to which income can be redistributed afterwards. In other words we need an incomes policy which deliberately seeks to narrow differentials. This is one reason for regretting the demise of the National Board for Prices and Incomes. It made a bold attempt to narrow differentials in its report on university teachers' salaries. But this policy was soon thwarted by bodies over which it had no control – particularly and finally by the Kindersley Committee, with its responsibilities for medical remuneration. But this is not the conclusion which is examined here.

The extent to which we can redistribute by selective benefits in favour of families with a head at work depends on the extent to which the reward for earning more can be reduced. Means-tested

*Brian Abel-Smith is Professor of Social Administration at the London School of Economics. Between 1968 and 1970 he was senior adviser to the Secretary of State for Social Services.

benefits such as family income supplement, rate and rent rebates and the new proposed rent allowances reduce the reward from extra earning as much as or more than earnings-related national insurance contributions and income tax. What is absurd about our present arrangement is that we are taking in income tax, national insurance and rates from the same families to whom we are offering help in means-tested benefits. And the fact that we are taking limits the extent to which we can give without the combined effect of giving and taking mechanisms removing all gain from extra work. Indeed, the more we take from poor families, the more we have to give. If we took less, we would have less need to give or could give more while leaving the same gain from extra earnings.

Thus, the starting point of this article is that to take less is as blessed as to give more – indeed, more blessed insofar as less stigma attaches to retaining what one has earned than to receiving what one has not. The mechanisms which take from poor families at work are, therefore examined to see how less can be taken.

At present a married couple with about average rent and rates amounting to £3.35 has to earn £16.40 to reach the poverty line,[1] simply because no less than £2.70 – over a sixth of earnings – has to be paid out in income tax and national insurance.[2] A 4-child family on the poverty line with a rent of £8 per week has to pay over £4 per week in income tax, national insurance and rates.

The largest single 'tax' on the poor at work is caused paradoxically by the attempt to relieve poverty among those not at work. A 2-child family on the poverty line with rent and rates of £3.35 pays £1.27 in national insurance contribution, and a family with 4 children £1.42. The less these families had to pay for national insurance, the more they would have to spend.

The present national insurance contribution still contains a

1. For brevity, the phrase 'poverty line' is used to indicate net income equivalent to the basic supplementary benefit scale for that family.
2. For brevity, the phrase 'national insurance' is used throughout to include industrial injury and the national health service contribution.

heavy flat-rate element. The distributional impact of insurance contributions was one reason why Beatrice Webb was so savagely opposed to national insurance. It is also what delighted some Tories in 1911. It seemed to at least one of them an excellent idea to make the poor pay for their own social services. The flat-rate national insurance contribution is, in fact, worse than a poll tax because it is not allowable as a deduction from income tax. Occupational pension contributions, mortgage payments and life insurance contributions can all be wholly or partly deducted from income before income tax is calculated. While these 'voluntary' payments are allowed, the compulsory national insurance contribution is currently not allowable.

In the national insurance contribution, virtually no account is taken of ability to pay. While those with very low incomes can claim exemption, this is not the same as the personal allowances in the income tax, which have the effect of providing the one remaining general source of progressive incidence up to the surtax threshold. The only apparent recognition of the principle of taxable capacity in the national insurance contribution is in the lower rates of contribution levied on juveniles and women, though the latter is usually explained by the fact that men receive benefits for more dependents than women do.

It is now, at last, common ground between the main political parties that contributions should eventually be earnings-related. Flat-rate contributions are to be abolished. The political debate now centres on the character and level of the benefits to which the compulsory earnings-related contributions will give title and, thus, on the level at which they will have to be set, particularly in the long run. While the Labour Party favours earnings-related pensions weighted to provide a high level of pension for the low earner, the Conservatives favour flat-rate pensions supplemented by occupational pensions with a 'fall-back' scheme for those not covered by an occupational scheme.

In the uprating of contributions and benefits (at a cost of £560 million in a full year), which took effect in September 1971, Sir Keith Joseph took a bold step towards earnings-related contributions. He left the level of flat-rate contribution unchanged,

He also left unchanged the rate charged on the band of earnings £9–£18 per week. A change in the rate charged on this band would have made it necessary for contracted-out occupational pension schemes to be readjusted. The whole of the money was raised by increasing the rate charged on earnings above £18 from 3.25 per cent to 4.35 per cent. As the revenue would have been inadequate if the ceiling of £30 for this band of contributions had been retained, the ceiling was raised to £42.

In distributional terms the incidence of the national insurance contribution, taken by itself, has been made less regressive. But regressive it remains. For an adult male who is not contracted out, the contribution amounts to 7.9 per cent of earnings of £15 per week, 6.2 per cent of earnings of £30 per week, and 5.6 per cent of earnings of £42 per week. But this is a transition to the wholly earnings-related contributions which the Government plans to introduce with its new arrangements for pensions in 1975. Ultimately, employees (other than married women and part-time workers with low earnings) in the new reserve pension scheme will have to pay 6¾ per cent of their earnings up to one and a half times average national earnings. Normally those in occupational pensions schemes will have to pay a higher percentage overall, but while their contribution of 5¼ per cent for the basic flat-rate scheme will not be allowed against tax, their further contribution to their occupational scheme will be deductible against income tax. A contribution of 6¾ per cent would lower the contribution of a married man with 2 children on the poverty line (£3.35 rent and rates) by 12 pence, and if he had 4 children, by 7 pence. To lighten the burden of national insurance on poor families, a more drastic change is needed than simply a switch to earnings-related contributions.

The Government proposes that employers should pay 9¾ per cent of earnings up to the contribution ceiling – thus abandoning the long established principle that employers and employees should pay roughly the same for social insurance. The burden on the low paid could be lightened still further by increasing the employers' share of the contribution, with a corresponding reduction in the employees' contribution. There are two main objections to this. First, the employers' contribution is probably passed on, in part at least, to export prices. Secondly, employers' contributions are probably passed on to consumers in higher prices at home. Insofar as they are, the switch from employees' to employers' earnings-related contributions would involve little more than a switch of the burden on poor families from direct to indirect taxation.

A second possibility is to use the existing Exchequer supplements to national insurance selectively to give further help to the lower paid. Among all the 'universal' benefits, the Exchequer subsidy of over £500 million to the national insurance fund has been curiously omitted from discussion of selectivity. Indeed, one could well ask what the Exchequer contribution is for. No specific answer to this question has been given for many years, other than the general statement that national insurance has always been on a tripartite basis. In recent years 'tripartite' has come to mean that the Exchequer should pay 18 per cent of total contribution income. Tripartite insurance was all very well when the higher paid were excluded from national insurance. But the principle of a *general* subsidy to national insurance can be questioned when over twelve million employees are covered by occupational pensions. It is true that certain risks, particularly unemployment and injury, arise to a greater extent among the lower paid, but it is many years since it was argued that the national insurance contribution should be adjusted to the risks of different socio-economic groups in the population.

Instead of being used as a general universal subsidy, the Exchequer contribution could be used to subsidize the contributions due from lower-paid workers, who are at present being assured of poverty at work in the attempt to save them from it when off work. In other words, the Exchequer's £500 million plus could be used to lower the rate of contribution paid from low earnings. For example, the present projected cost of national insurance could be paid for by a flat-rate contribution of only 25 pence, instead of 88 pence (not contracted-out) and a contribution of around 6½ per cent on earnings between £9 and £42 per week. A 2-child family on the poverty line would pay 50 pence less than at present and the saving for families with lower earnings would be greater still.

Alternatively, a notional flat rate of 10 pence could be levied on earnings up to £12 or £15 with a much higher rate on earnings subject to proportional contribution. The machinery is already in existence to charge different rates on different bands of income. A further possibility, though administratively more complicated, would be a contribution which took a decreasing percentage of each £1 of income below a certain level. This would however involve a marginal rate of contribution higher than the average rate, which would overlap with the existing marginal rate of taxation, loss of rate rebates, etc.

The essential point is that there is a variety of methods by which the burden of insurance contributions on the low paid could be lightened. Moreover, this could be done without undermining the essential principle of national insurance. Where a contributor was so poor that he could not afford the full cost of insurance, part of it would be paid by the Exchequer. In yet another way Exchequer help could be concentrated on those who needed it most. This is in line both with the Conservative election manifesto and with socialist principles. Moreover, while selective benefits have to be claimed, everyone would receive the advantage of the selective contribution automatically. It would achieve what many have hoped a negative income tax could achieve – a 'benefit' or weekly increase in income, based on the earnings of that week.

But all this assumes that the central principle of social insurance is to be retained – a definitive relationship between benefit and contribution. Indeed, it is this cardinal relation which makes a national insurance contribution distinguishable from a tax. Additional contribution must earn title to additional benefit. The Labour Government's proposed changes in national insurance were securely based on this principle. While the move from flat-rate to earnings-related contributions was intended to give relief to the lower-paid worker, the earnings-related benefit had a clear rationale and definitive purpose. The rationale was the need to reflect standards of living while at work in benefits paid when not at work. The purpose was to achieve in the long run levels of benefit which would make it unnecessary for all but a small minority to claim supplementary benefit. In this sense it was a plan to abolish poverty in the narrow sense among those off work.

The present Government has decided to abandon this key relationship between contribution and benefit. Flat-rate benefits are to be financed by earnings-related contributions. Once there is no acceptable relation between contribution and benefit, it ceases to be meaningful to use the word 'insurance'. The Government intends that future basic 'universal' social security benefits in Britain will be financed by what amounts to a social security tax.

The implications of this decision on the benefit rate are far-reaching. Flat-rate benefits will be left without any clear rationale. Those dependent on state pensions alone will still, even in the long run, have to claim supplementary benefit to keep out of poverty. So also will many with state pensions and occupational pensions. But it is the contributions which concern us here. It is because of the accepted relationship between benefit and contribution that so much money can be raised with so little criticism, either in Parliament or in the Press. Once this relationship is abandoned, governments will find it harder to raise the money needed for social and other public services. It is not only in Britain that the hypothetication of revenue for social insurance has added to the total revenue which governments are able to collect.

The virtual destruction of the insurance principle was recognized in Press comment on the 1971 budget. According to the *Daily Telegraph*, the contributor 'has never got proper value for his money and will now, under the new arrangements, get even less'. It continued its April Fool's Day editorial of 1971 with the sentence: 'The contribution is, in effect, a progressive [*sic*] form of direct taxation which bears most heavily on people of modest income.' Now that the Government has decided to finance social security from a social security tax, it must expect to be judged by the criteria normally applied in assessing the equity of a tax. It must also expect public opinion to regard it as a tax.

Taxation Policy

In its reform of income tax and surtax, the Government proposes to levy a proportional tax (provisionally set at 30 per cent) on a broad band of income. It is clearly not intended to reintroduce reduced rates of taxation, as the administrative simplicity of taxing at a proportional rate would be lost. Instead of favouring earned income by a special allowance there is to be a surcharge on investment income. This surcharge will, however, only apply above a certain level of investment income, so that the first slice of such income will be taxed at the rate applicable to earned income. In contrast, the new earnings-related contribution will only be levied on the *earned* income of employed persons. In total, therefore, the first slice of an employed person's earned income up to the personal tax threshold will be taxed by a reserve scheme insurance contribution of 6¾ per cent, and the next slice by a combined rate of 36¾ per cent (30 per cent plus 6¾ per cent). Finally, on earnings above one and a half times average earnings the rate will drop to 30 per cent. Those with investment income alone will not apparently be taxed at all up to the tax threshold as earnings-related contributions are not charged on investment income. When tax starts the rate will be 30 per cent, as distinct from 36¾ per cent if it were earned income. The rate will not rise above 30 per cent until the investment income surcharge starts to be paid. Thus, up to this point, those with unearned income will be less progressively taxed than those with earned income. It will be interesting to see how long such an inequitable arrangement will be retained.

Once the contributory principle is abandoned, there can be no justification for excluding investment income from the social security tax. New Zealand had such a tax until 1969 and it was on all income – both investment and earned income. Nor is there any reason for retaining a ceiling of income beyond which the tax is not payable. There had to be a ceiling in Labour's national superannuation scheme to preserve a fair relationship between contribution and benefit, and to cement the partnership with occupational pension schemes. Thirdly, there will be no justification for levying the tax on those too poor to pay it. It is true that the present national insurance contribution performs the administrative function of establishing title to benefit. It serves as evidence of whether people are or are not in the employment market and has a special importance in regulating title to benefit among part-time workers – particularly married women. But this administrative function does not require a contribution on the scale which is at present levied. It would be possible to secure the administrative objective by what would in effect be a work registration flat-rate contribution levied at the rate of say 10 pence per week. Thus, national insurance could be financed by a pay-roll tax on employers, a notional work-registration contribution paid by employees, and a higher rate of personal taxation levied on all income, both earned and unearned. The great advantage of this would be the extra income retained by poor families with a head at work. A family with 2 children at the present poverty level would gain over £1 a week. The families which benefited would be those that needed help most.

Thus, the burden of national insurance contributions on low earners could be substantially reduced, whatever the level of benefits or the relation between benefit and contribution. The logic of the Conservative Government's approach is for the bulk of contributions to be absorbed in a social security tax, forming part of the new personal income-tax. Labour's proposals for a high level of earnings-related pension related to contributions do not require high contributions from the lower paid. Exchequer subsidies could be used discriminately to lighten the burden on the low earner.

Income Tax

At present a married couple on the poverty line with about average rent and rates pays £1.48 per week in income tax. The 1971 budget excluded from income tax families below the poverty line, providing the rent and rates of a 2-child family did not exceed £3.45 per week and a 4-child family £4.10 per week. The present personal allowances for a single person and a married couple are far too low.

The tax threshold should be substantially above the poverty

line for those with average rent and rates, to allow for those whose rent and rates are abnormally high – particularly Londoners and those in furnished accommodation. A high tax threshold is required to leave room beneath it for the effects on marginal income of selective benefits and rebates. The tax threshold needs to be at least £600 for a single person and £800 for a married couple.

A rise in the tax threshold without any adjustment elsewhere in the system would be very costly. It would also be wasteful in distributional terms, as it would confer an equal benefit on all tax-payers – the rich as well as the poor. The advantage to the better-off could be easily counteracted by an increase in the rate of tax, but such an increase is unlikely to come from a government pledged to reduce rather than increase the tax on income. What other means are, therefore, available for limiting the impact on higher income groups and reducing the cost to a sum which can be relatively painlessly accommodated?

The personal allowances establish the minimum tax threshold. But the actual point at which different people start to pay tax varies enormously. This is because of the wide range of allowances which can be claimed. For example, a family with 1 child, earning £1,500 a year, which claims for an occupational pension contribution at the rate of 6½ per cent of earnings, life insurance relief of £25, and mortgage relief of £400, pays no tax – even though its income is well above the poverty line. These three forms of contractual saving establish tax thresholds which differ widely among families with the same income and family responsibilities. It is only people with no or very little contractual saving who are taxed into poverty.

Income tax hits hardest those who have no mortgage or cannot get one, those who are not in a contributory occupational pension scheme and those who have no life insurance – particularly those who cannot afford the premium. These three types of allowance for employees alone cost £487 million of revenue (income tax rates) – about a quarter of the Exchequer cost of the national health service. It is hard to find any convincing argument for this discrimination in favour of these forms of saving, other than that they have long existed and that commitments have been made on the assumption that they will continue. Occupational pensions are, of course, taxed when they are paid out, but normally only after tax-free income has been allowed to accumulate throughout working life.

The tax threshold could be discriminately raised for poorer families by allowing rent as an allowance against tax. Alternatively those in full-time work could be offered the option either of existing allowances or, mainly for those who cannot claim under these headings, new minimum personal allowances, which would raise the tax threshold for all at work to the level suggested above. The cost might be met by placing a money limit on the amount which could be claimed by any tax-payer under these three headings combined. Before one could give this type of proposal detailed consideration, one would need to know how much is claimed under these headings by what proportion of the population in different income groups.

Conclusion

Present policies are based on three conflicting principles. First, there is the principle of taxation according to ability to pay. This is the principle theoretically applied in income tax. But the Inland Revenue applies a harsher and less precise test of minimum requirements than the Supplementary Benefits Commission. Secondly, there is the principle of contributory insurance. People are compelled to insure against inability to earn, whether they can afford to do so or not. These policies in combination drive families at work into poverty or into deeper poverty. We have therefore developed a third set of policies – selective benefits and rebates, which pay back to the poor, in whole or in part, what the other two policies have taken away. The net result is to leave a residue of poverty, which can only apparently be relieved by depriving the poor of the opportunity to work their way out of poverty by earning more. If we take less, we will need to give less. Hence the need for a higher tax threshold. Hence also the need for the state to help pay the national insurance contributions of those who cannot afford to pay them themselves.

But our present conflicting principles are not solely due to uncoordinated policies. They are also due to conflicting values. Incentives are thought essential for the rich, but are ignored in the development of policies for the poor. People are taxed into poverty and then told to claim family income supplements to get back what has been taken away. 'Savings' in national insurance, which all at work are compelled to make, are not allowable against tax, while savings for life insurance, private pensions or house purchase, which only the better-off can afford to make, are allowable against tax. Only by a re-examination of these values can we provide the social security policies which society pretends to want without willing the means to pay.

13
Value-added Taxation

DAVID STOUT*

In economic affairs there can hardly ever be a course of action –
whether it involves intervention or refusal to intervene – which is free
from drawbacks. It is for the government to decide whether the balance of advantage for the nation would justify them in submitting a
proposal for legislation to Parliament. – Green Paper on Regional
Employment Premium

To tax and to please, no more than to love and to be wise, is not
given to man. – Edmund Burke

Value-added taxation is a method of imposing an *ad valorem* tax
on final consumer spending within the domestic economy. The
whole of the sales value of consumer goods and services, whether
imported or produced at home, is taxed by instalments as the
goods pass along the production and distribution chain involving
successive transactions between businesses. Although the tax is
levied at all stages, their total value is subject to tax once and once
only. Under the 'invoice' system, each business pays the tax as a
percentage (the VAT rate) of its sales during the preceding tax
period (say a quarter), but *less* a credit for the VAT invoiced to
it over that period by its own suppliers. There are of course no
tax-invoice credits for the final consumer – nor, for that matter,
for any tax-exempt business purchaser (like the farmer, say, if
food and farming activities are treated as tax-exempt). For these
purchasers, there is *no* recovery of pre-paid tax: the buck stops
there.

Export sales are completely freed from the VAT of the
country that produces them. However the purchased inputs into

*The author is a Fellow of University College, Oxford, a senior lecturer
in economics in Oxford University, and Economic Director of the National
Economic Development Office.

these exports are all free of VAT, since the exporter is kept within the VAT net. He is treated like a VAT-payer who is subject to a zero rate of tax on his exports and so he can claim and enjoy a credit for the tax invoiced to him on his purchases.

It can be seen that 'value added' is a misnomer. Domestic value added, in the economist's sense, is approximated by taking total domestic expenditure on consumption and investment goods (including the value of the physical increase in stocks), adding exports, subtracting imports and subtracting the depreciation of the capital stock over the year. Value added for tax purposes excludes net capital formation. (Sales of capital goods are subject to VAT, but the invoiced tax is credited to the purchaser, with no corresponding production of consumer goods and services within that tax period.) It also excludes exports, but includes imports. The base is therefore home consumption.[1] VAT is in fact a multi-stage consumption tax with no overspill into exports, capital investment or business costs. It can therefore be sharply contrasted both with the hydrocarbon oil duties and with selective employment tax, and also, but less starkly, with purchase tax, some 13 per cent or so of the revenue of which accrues from business purchases. These latter taxes, insofar as they are reflected in the prices of the goods and services they enter, which themselves are incorporated in other goods subject to taxes like purchase tax, lead to double taxation and a milder version of the cascading problem that Continental countries experienced under their old cumulative-turnover tax-regimes.

1. Because of the tax credit mechanism, VAT is emphatically not – as some commentators have alleged – a tax on '*costs* and consumption'. See, e.g., J. Bracewell-Milnes, 'VAT in the UK', *Journal of Business Finance*, autumn 1968, p. 22. For a detailed description of VAT see NEDO, *Value-added Tax*, 2nd edition, April 1971, Chap. 2. There is a briefer description in the Green Paper on *Value-added Tax*, HMSO, Cmnd. 4621, March 1971; and in D. Stout, 'Economic Aspects of a Value-added Tax in the UK', in Rybczynski (ed.), *The Value-added Tax: the UK Position and European Experience*, Basil Blackwell, 1969.

Some General Considerations

We are shortly to introduce VAT into our taxation system in place of purchase tax and selective employment tax. Much of the argument about VAT has so far been about the costs and problems of its administration and about the possible change in the general level of prices when it is introduced. These questions are interesting and important, but they are not fundamental. What matters is that VAT is a 'European' tax and radically different from what we have come to think of as 'British' taxes. It springs from a conscious effort to achieve *neutrality* in indirect taxation. The abandonment of a selective tax like purchase tax and the embracing of a VAT (even with exemptions and even if with multiple rates) is a logical first step towards a system of taxes which brings (as closely as possible while still raising revenue) relative prices into line with relative costs throughout the markets of the countries adopting VAT.

It is far from certain whether Western Europe will take more than this large first step in the foreseeable future. So long as VAT is levied at different rates in different countries; so long as governments recognize a duty to influence the distribution of economic rewards through the progressive taxation of income; so long as other indirect taxes single out particular goods for protection, discouragement or convenient charge; so long as governments spend the proceeds of taxation on a different basket of goods from the one the tax-payers themselves would have chosen: then so long will our system of taxation and public spending continue to influence prices and affect economic choice.

It is inconceivable that we shall ever cease to use the taxation system, in part at least, as a way of discriminating between persons and between activities. Governments are elected because of commonly held views about goods which are desirable in general but which individuals cannot be relied upon to seek in particular. Social justice cannot be entrusted to charities. Also, there are economic goals which can never be achieved through the individual's search for gain. Certain economic decisions bring important benefits or costs to other groups than those participating directly in the decision. Governments will seek to bring these 'externalities' into account. They may do this either by direct intervention or by designing a framework of taxation to equate, so far as is practicable, the private and public benefits of different decisions. But where there are no *clear* grounds for discriminating, neutrality is no bad principle.

Some of the confusion in the debates about tax policy arises because the *same* tax change may be defended on the ground that it seeks to get rid of discrimination where discrimination is thought not to improve the social consequences of private choice; and on the ground that it *does* so discriminate. SET was at one time defended on the grounds that it brought services into the tax net and achieved a greater measure of neutrality than was possible with a purchase tax on certain goods by itself. But it was also defended on the ground that the social return from employment of labour and capital in the services sector was less than the return from their employment in manufacturing, because of the relationship that was alleged to hold between the rate of growth of productivity in the economy as a whole and the size of the manufacturing sector.

The presumption in favour of neutrality in the taxation system has gathered strength, both on the Continent and more recently and less dramatically here and in the United States, from a growing conviction that some taxes, in particular some taxes on expenditure and taxes on corporations, have discriminated arbitrarily. They have marked out goods, activities and organizations, but not in such a way as to equalize personal income or to increase the social product.

The most glaring example was the varying burden of taxation on different goods under 'cascade' turnover taxes in a number of Continental countries. The more separate, unintegrated stages of production a good passed through, the more times the same value added at early stages was subject to tax. It is hard for tax-payers in a country like ours with little experience of the extreme anomalies from spill-over of multi-stage taxation to appreciate the almost universal acclaim with which VAT was greeted in Germany in 1968.

But there are less obvious examples too. Professor Harberger has led a considerable campaign over many years in the United States against the selection of corporate profits (rather than corporate value-added) as the base of corporate taxation. To do this, he argues, is to discriminate wantonly against the use of capital in the productive process. Corporate income-taxation interferes with the criteria for selecting a method of production and so imposes an excess burden on the economy. Redistribution of the proceeds of capital-using enterprise in the hands of individuals is properly dealt with not by cutting off the roots of the tree but by dividing the fruit. This argument certainly sounds more relevant as living standards rise, and as institutional saving spreads shareholding more widely. It is a point of view which leads towards the taxation of personal income and personal realized capital gains; and towards value added rather than profits alone as the basis of business taxation.

In Britain the adoption of a VAT may be defended on the ground that, itself a neutral tax, it may replace some other taxes which *arbitrarily* discriminate,[2] or which, beyond their present level, would seriously distort choice or stifle effort and initiative. When the tax replaces our two principal indirect taxes on goods and services (other than the specific duties), it is necessary also to show that where the existing taxes discriminate, they do not systematically make income distribution fairer or bring social and private returns closer together. Alternatively, it would need to be shown that where the present taxes do have a desirable effect, this effect could be better achieved within the whole structure of taxes and government transfer payments and spending, without selecting out particular goods or particular categories of employee.

Recent History of VAT

VAT is surely the world's fastest growing tax. Shortly after the war the Shoup tax mission to Japan recommended the adoption of a wide-ranging VAT to assist Japanese economic recon-

2. The high rate of purchase tax on TV sets, for instance, adversely affects income distribution.

struction. In spite of clear and careful argument the tax was not adopted. By 1955 France had reformed her turnover tax system, adopting value-added taxation. By 1965 value-added tax was to be found only in France (up to the wholesale stage) and in the State of Michigan. Six years later, VAT is a major source of revenue all the way to the retail stage in France, Germany, Belgium, the Netherlands, Luxembourg, Denmark, Norway and Sweden and is shortly to be introduced as part of major revisions of indirect taxes in Italy, Ireland and the United Kingdom.[3] In 1970 the study of VAT in the United States as a Federal (revenue-sharing) tax which would not enter the price of exports, as many other Federal taxes do, proceeded as far as the preparation of a draft bill for consideration by the Administration which did not, however, submit it to Congress.

This pandemic, as some would regard it, is principally due to the adoption in 1967 by the Council of Ministers of the EEC of two directives designed to harmonize indirect taxation in the member states on the basis of VAT. For members and potential members of the Community a VAT thus became *de rigueur*. For other countries, its adoption by the EEC countries meant that some of their important trading rivals would be able to meet increasing government revenue needs out of a tax which was levied entirely upon consumption, including imports, and not at all upon the labour and capital of intermediate inputs entering exports.

In the United Kingdom the earliest serious study of the tax was undertaken by economists working for the National Economic Development Office under Sir Robert Shone's inspiration in the summer of 1962. We were at that time casting about for a change in the tax system which might help to remove some of the obstacles to faster economic growth. Attention was focused upon the possible replacement of part of corporation tax by a VAT as a paradigm case of a neutral indirect tax. This tax change, together with a net wealth tax to meet the social objections to a general consumption tax, formed the basis of Chapter E, the

3. The Continental developments are described in detail in NEDO, op. cit., Chap. 4.

taxation chapter of the famous Orange Book submitted to the NED Council early in 1963.[4]

The next development, however, pushed VAT back into the shadows. In his 1963 budget speech the Chancellor, Mr Maudling, announced the setting-up of the Richardson Committee to investigate the practical effects of introducing a tax of this kind. An Addington Society conference at which Professor Kaldor, Professor Prest, Professor Wheatcroft and the writer presented papers, provided a dress-rehearasal for some of the theoretical and administrative argument before the Richardson Committee.[5] This Committee rejected the arguments for reducing the scope of direct taxes, and for introducing a VAT when it reported in 1964.

In the next two years it became clear that the EEC would adopt a VAT and that, in some form, a VAT would almost certainly be a necessary condition of entry. The Richardson Report had not satisfactorily settled the question of the economic effects of a change in the tax structure away from direct taxes towards neutral indirect taxes. In June 1966 the NED Council set up a committee to re-examine VAT. This committee included representatives from the Confederation of British Industry, the Trades Union Congress and the NED Office. It considered the economic and social implications of a VAT in two contexts: as an alternative to part of corporation tax (or to an *increase* in corporation tax); and as an alternative to purchase tax and SET. Visits were paid to Denmark, France, Germany and the Netherlands to examine the practical application of the tax in those countries. The most important innovation was a detailed survey of industrial views through the Economic Development Committees and other industry committees. The Report was published by the Office in August 1969.

4. NEDC, *Conditions Favourable to Faster Growth*, paras. 163–70. The tax was described as an illustration of 'the type of tax changes which might encourage growth'. The publication of the report was authorized by the Council on 5 April 1963.

5. These papers were published in *British Tax Review*, Sept.–Oct. 1963.

The Report observed that it was not its purpose
to draw conclusions or to make recommendations about whether or not
it would be desirable to introduce a VAT in this country. It aims to
set out some of the main considerations which would be involved if a
VAT *were* to be considered as a possibility. Before this could happen
one prior question would need to be answered: do we wish to increase
the proportion of revenue raised by a broadly based *ad valorem* tax on
consumption, in preference to increasing direct taxation on individuals
or companies, or to raising existing more narrowly based or specific
indirect taxes? If the answer to this question is Yes, then a VAT takes
its place alongside other possibilities, such as a more comprehensive
purchase tax, a general sales tax or perhaps variants of a pay-roll tax
and the SET ... So far as a VAT is concerned, it *would* automatically include the services sector, it *could* include retailing, and it
would avoid the problem of spill-over. Against this would need to be
set the certainty of its greater administrative complexity, the prob-
ability of a rise in prices, and the possibility of some regressive impact
which would require correction.[6]

I come back to these last two questions later. It was made clear
in the body of the Report that the effect upon the general level of
prices and upon the distribution of real income depended upon a
comparison of the mixture of taxes including a VAT with the
mixture excluding VAT, upon the rate or rates at which VAT
was imposed, including the scope and method of exemptions,
and upon the understanding by business decision-takers and
consumers of the resulting changes in the burden of tax upon
different activities.

In the 1971 budget, the Chancellor announced that he proposed to abolish both purchase tax and SET by April 1973 and
to introduce, in their place, a broadly based VAT, with relief for
food, farming, housing, finance, health, education, books, newspapers, periodicals, and charities. The mechanism of the VAT
was briefly outlined in the Green Paper already referred to.

What of the future of VAT? It is the long-term aim of the
Community to harmonize both indirect and direct taxes as a
complement to the removal of tariff and other barriers between
member countries. In that event, VAT would cease to be levied

6. NEDO, *Value-added Tax*, HMSO, August 1969 (and April 1971),
paras. 1.21 and 1.23.

according to the 'country of destination' principle upon domestic consumption but would be levied on domestic production within countries of origin. It is difficult to imagine this day of total tax harmonization ever dawning. The tax is at present levied in Europe at a bewildering variety of rates, ranging from a standard rate of 10 per cent and a reduced rate of 5 per cent in Luxembourg, an across-the-board rate of 15 per cent with almost no exemptions in Denmark, to 4 separate rates in France ranging from 7.5 per cent to 33.3 per cent and with many exemptions. The unweighted average standard rate is 16 per cent but there are few signs of any conscious central tendency of particular countries towards this figure. Rates have tended to creep up and it seems likely that a standard rate of about 20 per cent will eventually be typical.

The Balance of Direct and Indirect Taxation

The whole structure of direct and indirect taxes and public expenditure should be designed to reach an acceptable compromise between a number of different objectives of economic and social policy. The principal objectives relate to the provision of public goods, to equity, to the control of demand and the achievement of reasonably full employment without unreasonable inflation, to the efficient allocation of resources, and to the encouragement of economic growth. It is vain to try to evaluate any particular tax from all these points of view; and consequently many of the debates about particular taxes are sterile. Reasonable men differ about the importance of different partly conflicting objectives (like equity and incentives). The objectives are fulfilled or not by the whole set of taxes, transfer payments and public expenditure, and not by earmarking individual taxes or payments for particular purposes. And the powers of government extend far beyond taxation, to monetary policy, direct controls, planning mechanisms and institutions, international treaties and consultation at many levels within the economy.

What, if anything, can we say about the desirable balance between direct and indirect taxation, for example? By international standards, the proportion of total taxation levied on purchases or transactions is quite high in the United Kingdom. At 47 per cent, excluding social security contributions, our ratio in 1968 in OECD industrial countries ranked second only to Denmark.[7] But within this total, local rates and specific revenue duties on three types of commodity – tobacco, alcoholic drinks and hydro-carbon oils – bulked very large indeed. The three duties accounted for a much larger proportion of indirect taxation (42 per cent) than in any other OECD industrial country. *Ad valorem* taxes on consumption are rather low in the UK and indirect taxes levied on businesses without rebate – in particular the oil duties, SET and a small part of the purchase tax – are high. So within the family of indirect taxes we number some important members which have as close an affinity to direct taxes upon businesses as to taxes on personal expenditure. They bear on the costs of capital goods and exports and will tend to be reflected in the prices of these goods. Corporation tax bears on profits on these goods and may also be reflected, in the long run, in their prices.

The difference between direct and indirect taxes is purportedly between taxes which are ultimately borne by the object of the tax and those which are supposed to be shifted from the immediate object elsewhere, forwards to the consumer or backwards to the employee. It is evident, when studies are made of actual tax changes, that the incidence of a tax is not something that comes with it, like a price-tag: it depends upon all the circumstances of its introduction, including the state of competition between the tax-payers, the coincidental changes in other taxes, the rate at which the tax is levied and the degree of understanding of the tax in the community. It is different both in the short run and in the long run.

There are circumstances, in fact, in which the substitution of a fairly comprehensive uniform VAT for part of corporation tax would result in VAT-exclusive prices no lower than before and a dilution of the benefits to producers of exports and import-substitutes (who might distribute their additional after-tax profits instead of devoting them to competitive efforts). The benefit to

7. NEDO, op. cit., Chap. 3, Table 8.

the more efficient producers may also be much reduced, and the benefit to the firm contemplating a large investment outlay may disappear.

There are circumstances in which the change could set off a chain reaction of increased (VAT-inclusive) prices, wage settlements and industrial costs, so that our exports and import-substitutes would be actually disadvantaged. But there are other circumstances (wide differences between competing firms in the ratio of profits to value added; the seizing of competitive advantages by the more profitable firms; pressures leading to time-lags in the recommendation of higher retail prices; awareness of the effects upon the present value of expansionary investment of *markedly* lower corporate tax rates) when such a change might carry with it unalloyed benefits to the economy. It is not the tax changes themselves that one should judge but all the circumstances of their introduction.

If the balance between a general consumption tax and corporate income tax is looked at, the question of adjusting the distribution of income only arises to the extent that dividend distributions are affected.

If what we are considering is a change in the taxation structure which substitutes a general consumption tax like VAT for part of corporation tax, and at a rate which maintains the real value of the budget surplus after all consequent changes in tax yields and the cost of government goods are taken into account, then we can expect that the change in the distribution of real personal income is likely to be small, and not to require as much attention as when we are considering a change within the system of taxes on consumption away from selectivity and towards generality. Quite large changes in the taxation of corporate profits over long periods of time make little detectable difference to the shares of profits and wages and salaries in income after tax. The 'contribution' of corporate profits tax per £ of final demand will vary a little from industry to industry. But if these tax changes are reflected in prices they are unlikely systematically to disadvantage consumers with low incomes, particularly not if compensating reductions are also made in non-corporate (including farm) incomes. If an increase in income inequality were to arise it would very possibly be small enough to be corrected by quite minor increases in family allowances or a small element of negative income tax.

The principal danger of increasing the relative importance of *ad valorem* consumption taxes at the expense of the yield from corporate income tax is lest the circumstances of the change prevent any overall reduction of VAT-*exclusive* prices.

In the very long run, the benefits that may result from a switch of business taxation from direct to indirect, or that may be thwarted by a consequent increase of prices, are of vanishing importance. They matter no more than would a 2 or 3 per cent devaluation for example, whether outflanked or not by a consequent increase in domestic costs. This benefit, if enjoyed, is transient, but the change in the structure of taxation that caused it is as permanent as anything can be in the field of economic policy. Hence the important questions are perhaps about the merits and disadvantages of alternative systems of levying taxes indefinitely, rather than about the once-and-for-all effects of a switch.

These questions can best be asked about alternative systems of indirect taxation, and they draw us back to the permanent effects of alternative systems upon the allocation of resources; to the political philosophy of 'neutrality' in indirect taxation; to the convenience of one system or the other from the point of view of regional discrimination, revenue buoyancy, and regulation of demand; and to ease our complexity of administration. They may also draw us to the broader questions of income distribution, though we should recognize that the immediate differences that may seem to be entailed by different indirect tax structures are likely to be swamped, in the long run, by more fundamental political determinants of relative incomes after all taxes and benefits; by methods of wage determination; and by the effects of industrial structure and international competition upon pricing and ease of entry. I shall consider very briefly each of these questions in the present context: namely the replacement of purchase tax and SET by a VAT, with certain exemptions, at a rate assumed to provide the same yield to the government.

Neutrality and Resource Allocation

A uniform, comprehensive VAT is neutral in four respects. Firstly, it is neutral between different goods and services. This is a virtue if one believes that consumers are the best judges of what to consume, that the degree of monopoly is everywhere the same, and that there are no important external benefits or detriments resulting from the consumption of particular goods. There may be good grounds for plumping for selectivity, for example where the consumption of particular goods – such as cigarettes or private motor transport – is regarded as detrimental either to the consumer or to other members of the community. Wherever selectivity introduces arbitrary distinctions between goods or penalizes goods and activities which are not obviously harmful, there is a lot to be said for dispensing with such discrimination and preferring the neutrality of a VAT to cover most cases, employing specific duties or licence fees to deal with exceptional cases. There is no very clear logic about our present system, which subjects gramophone records to 55 per cent purchase tax and bicycles to 36⅔ per cent, but leaves pianos and yachts free of tax.

Secondly, a VAT is neutral between businesses. In this respect it differs both from purchase tax and from SET which treat differently companies with establishments engaged in manufacturing and in distribution.[8] It differs also from corporation tax and income tax, which assess incorporated business and unincorporated business on different bases.

Thirdly, a VAT is neutral between different methods of production and distribution. To a small extent purchase tax, and to a much larger extent hydrocarbon oil duties, are levied without rebate on industrial inputs, and corporation tax is levied on the profits of producers of capital goods, again without rebate to the user of these goods. In distribution, SET provides a contrary bias in favour of capital-intensive activity or the use of less but more highly skilled labour. Again, there may be special reasons

8. Not to mention establishments engaged in pasteurizing milk on the one hand and freezing vegetables on the other.

for wanting to influence the choice of technique. But on general grounds, this would normally be towards more capital-intensive techniques (for example because the rate of diffusion of new techniques and the underlying rate of technical progress itself depended in part upon the rate of investment). On balance, one is likely to get a little closer to this by increasing dependence upon a broadly based VAT.

Fourthly, unless there are special reasons to the contrary, one may seek equality of tax treatment of imports and home-produced consumer goods (though, short of international tax harmonization, this goal is never fully achievable). VAT, like most but not all of purchase tax, but unlike SET, makes this possible insofar as country-of-destination taxes are concerned.

If neutrality is in general desired (and it may not be), then it is important to consider why the scope of a single-stage tax like purchase tax should not be extended instead. There are good reasons based upon the problems of policing revenue at the retail stage, upon the administrative impossibility, without accounts quite as detailed as those required for a VAT, of avoiding spill-over into exports and capital investment and double-taxation problems. There is also the danger that the general level of prices will rise more sharply if at some future time a *single-stage* tax is increased and a (multi-stage) direct tax reduced.[9]

When we come to consider goods versus services as a whole, substitution of a VAT for both purchase tax and SET will probably make very little difference, since SET largely removed a bias in favour of services that purchase tax had created. What we had were two selective taxes, one based upon the wholesale value of goods, the other based on the quantity of labour in services. It is not easy to defend them in the face of the general indirect tax alternative. Before SET was introduced, it would have been possible to justify the substitution of VAT for pur-

9. These points are dealt with in detail in NEDO, op. cit. (2nd edition) paras. 5, 59 to 5, 79. The possibility of basing VAT on the model of a purchase tax, with early transaction under suspension of tax, is discussed and rejected in 5, 93–5, 101.

chase tax on similar grounds to those used by Professor Reddaway, *ex post facto*, in justifying SET.[10]

Regulation of Demand

It is important for a chancellor to possess within his tool-kit of taxes and benefits some instruments that can be applied very quickly as well as some which automatically tend to stabilize demand. The advantage of possessing what Mr Selwyn Lloyd first called a 'regulator' is not so great as possessing the second sight required to enable one to know when to use it. Nonetheless it would be imprudent not to have such an instrument. Purchase tax, together with the specific duties, has been principally relied on in the past, though – not surprisingly in an economy with an inflationary bias – the regulator has in practice been used mainly to turn off the taps, not to turn them on.[11]

What can be said about a VAT on this score? The wider the base of indirect taxes and the less discriminatory the rates of tax on particular goods, the less likely it is that an increase in the rates will fail to lower consumption but simply divert it towards untaxed or less taxed goods and services. Conversely, the narrower the range of taxed goods the larger must be the rise in taxation and relative price (and the greater the excess burden of the tax) to achieve any given reduction in consumption. In the case of a comprehensive VAT, there is nothing that can be substituted except savings and holidays abroad, both of which may be what the doctor ordered! Furthermore, to reduce the dependence of the regulator upon beer and cigarettes is dramatically to reduce its incidence upon people with low incomes.

10. Professor W. B. Reddaway: *Effects of the Selective Employment Tax, First Report: the Distributive Trades*, HMSO, 1970.

11. In times of 'cost-push' inflation regulatory changes in indirect taxes can have paradoxical effects. Increases may immediately reduce real demand; but eventually, because of the rise in the cost of living, lead to higher money wage settlements and increases in domestic costs. cf. Peacock and Williamson, 'Consumption Taxes and Compensatory Finance', *Economic Journal*, March 1967. The 'regulator' is likely to be forsworn in these times, when inflation and high unemployment go hand in hand.

Unlike a change in purchase tax, a change in VAT will quite swiftly have an impact upon the prices, demands, and liquidity of producers far upstream of the purchase tax stage.

On the other hand, just because so very many more tax-payers (more than 1 million instead of about 65,000) have to adjust their invoicing or reset their accounting machines when the VAT rate is changed, chancellors may seek to avoid or to postpone changes for administrative reasons. (It is not an adequate answer to this objection that the regulator has in any case been used very sparingly during its lifetime.)

Income Distribution and the Introduction of a VAT

There is no space here to do anything like justice to this contentious question. Broadly, the facts appear to be that while purchase tax on motorcars is clearly still progressive, purchase tax as a whole is not clearly progressive; SET, if reflected in the prices of foodstuffs in the shops, for example, may be slightly regressive; and the present system of indirect taxation as a whole, including the specific duties, is regressive to an extent that broadly offsets the progressiveness of the *direct* taxes over quite a wide range of incomes. It is therefore fair to say that most of the redistribution in the system comes about by way of the disposition of benefits and not the total structure of taxes.[12]

If we assume that all three taxes are fully shifted, then the substitution of VAT for purchase tax and SET, with food exempted, and hypothetically at an equal yielding rate, would only slightly increase the inequality of income[13] before any changes in the pattern of demand or adjustments in wages are allowed

12. See the celebrated analysis by Merrett and Monk, *Bulletin of O.U. Institute of Economics and Statistics*, August 1966; and the studies of income distribution published from time to time in *Economic Trends*, (most recently in February 1971, pp. ix–xliv).

13. Assuming certain consequential tax changes, Professor Brown has calculated (in PEP, *Impact of Tax Changes on Income Distribution*, 1971) that the sufferers would be middle-income families with gains registered at the top and bottom ends of the spectrum. As Mr Dominick Harrod put it, echoing the peers in *Iolanthe*, 'Bow, bow, ye lower middle classes ...!' (*Daily Telegraph*, 12 February 1971.)

for. It is worth observing that, following the model of the draft American bill, it would not be impossible to levy VAT at a single rate (with the exemptions of foodstuffs, farmers, housing, finance, health, education, charities and newspapers, books and periodicals, as foreshadowed in the Green Paper) in such a way as to make the entire system of taxes and benefits a good deal more progressive than it is at present. This could be done by levying VAT at a higher rate than required to replace the present yield of SET and the 1973 projected yield of purchase tax, and paying back the difference in the form of *per capita* consumption allowances. On rough calculations, the money value of the 1973 base with the exclusions listed and deducting also the present specific duties (on the assumption that they would be adjusted downwards so that the effective rate of tax on these goods, including VAT, remained the same) as well as SET and purchase tax, would be about £17,500 million. The money yield of the two existing indirect taxes would then be compensated for by a VAT at about 13 per cent. If, for the sake of argument, VAT were to be levied at a rate 7 per cent higher, the theoretical yield would increase by something approaching £1,200 million. If this were redistributed in the form of consumption allowances of £20 per head, set against an assumed consumption of £120 of taxed goods and services for every man, woman and child (equivalent to the first £210 of consumption of an average mixed basket of taxed and exempt goods) then a significant additional element of progression would be introduced into the system by what amounts to its combination with a negative poll tax. The table below shows effective resulting ratios of net VAT to con-

VAT as Percentage of Disposable Income

Family size	Income level (£)			
	1,000	2,000	3,000	4,000
Single person	7.5%	8.5%	8.8%	9.0%
Married couple	5.5%	7.5%	8.2%	8.5%
Couple with 1 child	3.5%	6.5%	7.5%	8.0%
Couple with 2 children	1.5%	5.5%	5.1%	7.5%

sumption, assuming that the whole of disposable income is consumed for families of different size and levels of income. The upper limit approached by high income families is 9.5 per cent, or 20 per cent of the average ratio of taxed to untaxed goods.

The arithmetic of this example assumes that exempt goods are wholly freed from tax, which is unlikely in practice. But there is probably an element of 'overkill' in the example. Perhaps a rebate of something closer to £350 million, i.e. the tax on rather less than £50 per head of taxed goods per year, would more than restore the pre-existing degree of inequality. This would entail a VAT of about 15 per cent.

Conclusion

The substitution of approximate neutrality (with the exceptions provided) for selectivity in our indirect tax system will have a number of effects that in the past have been keenly sought after abroad and generally despised in this country. We should remember that so far as concerns the vital issue of social justice, what matters is not the impact of one tax in isolation, with its final resting-place prejudged, but the effect of the entire system of taxes, non-tax changes, public spending, and transfer payments upon the distribution of income, after allowing for probable tax-shifting.

On the side of growth and the efficient allocation of resources, there is no doubt that VAT has some merit compared with purchase tax and SET, which fall partly upon exports and investment, and compared with the alternative of higher rates of corporation tax and personal income tax. We cannot prejudge the extent to which such benefits may be eroded by inflation or counter-balanced in the short term by administrative difficulties. But it is clearly vitally important to design and publicize and present the tax change in such a way as to minimize these risks.

MORE ABOUT PENGUINS
AND PELICANS

Penguinews, which appears every month, contains details of all the new books issued by Penguins as they are published. From time to time it is supplemented by *Penguins in Print*, which is a complete list of all available books published by Penguins. (There are well over three thousand of these.)

A specimen copy of *Penguinews* will be sent to you free on request, and you can become a subscriber for the price of the postage. For a year's issues (including the complete lists) please send 30p if you live in the United Kingdom, or 60p if you live elsewhere. Just write to Dept EP, Penguin Books Ltd, Harmondsworth, Middlesex, enclosing a cheque or postal order, and your name will be added to the mailing list.

Note: *Penguinews* and *Penguins in Print* are not available in the U.S.A. or Canada

IN DEFENCE OF POLITICS

Bernard Crick

'One of the most thoughtful products of the political dialogues of the London School of Economics since the great days of Tawney, Dalton, Wallas, and Hobhouse. Its sobriety, liberal spirit, and toughness of mind are rare qualities in any political work' – *Guardian*

At a time of brittle cynicism about the activities of politicians, this essay, which has been specially revised for Penguins, makes 'an attempt to justify politics in plain words by saying what it is'. In a civilized community, which is no mere tribe, the establishment among rival groups and interests of political order – of agreed rules for the game – marks the birth of freedom. In spite of the compromises, deals, half-measures, and bargains which prompt impatient idealists to regard politics as a dirty word – indeed, because of them – the negotiating processes of politics remain the only tested alternative to government by outright coercion.

'Original and profound. It is hard to think of anyone interested in politics at any level who would not benefit by reading it' – Max Beloff in the *Daily Telegraph*

WESTERN CAPITALISM SINCE THE WAR

Michael Kidron

Western economic expansion since the War has been staggering. 'High employment, fast economic growth and stability are now considered as normal . . . and half the working population have known nothing else.' What are the reasons for this economic boom? And how likely is it to last?

Michael Kidron suggests that this phenomenon is not primarily a result of governmental planning, increased international trade, or scientific innovations in industry, but of the size of the arms budget. However, despite the veneer of affluence afforded by the arms economy, he sees the stability of western capitalism as seriously threatened by the number of problems it has nurtured. In the light of this diagnosis, Kidron examines in detail the economic situation as affected by prices and wages controls, international currency arrangements, trade unions, and parliamentary reform.

Described in *New Society* as 'an important book, immensely topical and intelligent', Michael Kidron's challenging and controversial theory must be of interest to politician, economist, and layman alike.

BRITISH CAPITALISM, WORKERS AND THE PROFITS SQUEEZE

Andrew Glyn and Bob Sutcliffe

According to the authors of this provocative Penguin Special, British capitalism has in the last few years given the lie to the basic assumption of the great majority of Western economists. Work-force's share of the economic cake, like that of Profit, remains more or less constant. They see the implications to be revolutionary, in a literal sense.

They analyse the situation as follows. Because of increasing international competition, firms have been unable to pass on as higher prices the increased wages they have been forced to concede. Profit margins have narrowed. The evidence is clear and plentiful. But without profit to finance dividends and reinvestment, capitalism cannot survive. So which will be sacrificed – the System itself or the prosperity of ninety per cent of the population? Either way the political consequences will be formidable.

A Penguin Special

A DICTIONARY OF POLITICS

Florence Elliott

Sixth Edition Completely Revised

This guide to modern politics has been fully revised and contains entries on such recent developments as the latest independent states of Africa and the Caribbean. It provides a comprehensive and informative background to current events and includes life histories of the world's leading politicians. The political institutions, recent history, and economy of almost every independent state in the world are discussed. There are entries on important overseas possessions and places which are, or have been, centres of dispute. The aims of some of the major political parties of the world are explained. International organizations are described. Political beliefs and dates of many important declarations, pacts and treaties are clearly set out. Cross-references have been included where further explanation might help the reader to a better understanding of the subject under discussion.

A Penguin Reference Book

PRINCIPLES OF POLITICAL ECONOMY AND TAXATION

David Ricardo

Though Adam Smith founded the first 'school' of economic thought, now known as Classical Economics, it was David Ricardo's *Principles* that provided it with an elaborate and sophisticated textbook. In the introduction to this edition R. M. Hartwell shows how Ricardo still tended to explain the wealth of a nation, even in 1817, in agricultural, mercantile and financial terms (to the exclusion of industrial production). Nonetheless his *Principles* presented an interpretation of economic activity which reigned supreme for half a century and is still a useful tool of analysis for certain problems today.

A Pelican Classic

Another Pelican edited by
William A. Robson and Bernard Crick

THE FUTURE OF THE SOCIAL SERVICES

What are our priorities in the social services? We cannot do all that needs to be done. What shall we do? What shall we leave undone?

In this collection of articles assembled by the editors of *Political Quarterly* distinguished social scientists and and social workers consider the future of the social services in a changing world. The following subjects are considered:

The Role of the Social Services
Universality Versus Selectivity
Civic Rights and Social Services
Housing Policies and Prospects
Public Involvement in Planning
Education as a Social Service
The Future of Community Development
The Future of the Personal Social Services
The Seebohm Report
A Facelifting for the N.H.S. – a Major or a Minor Operation?
Pensions Reform
Which Social Services Can We Save?
Economic Priority: Growth or Welfare?